High-Net-Worth Psychology

Finding, Winning and Keeping Affluent Investors

Russ Alan Prince
Karen Maru File

High-Net-Worth Psychology

by Russ Alan Prince and Karen Maru File

HNW Press

HNW Press
76 Penfield Road
Fairfield CT 06430
Tel: 203-255-8772
Fax: 203-256-9147
Printed in the United States of America. Printing number 1.
ISBN number 0-9658391-3-3

Cover and book design by Luna Corporate Design
Tel. 203-378-2543 email LunaCorp@aol.com

Other books by the authors:
Russ Alan Prince and Karen Maru File

Published by HNW Press (203-255-8772)
Prince Winning the War for the Wealthy: How Life Insurance Companies Can Dominate the Upscale Markets (1999)
Prince, Rathbun, File The Perfect Legacy: Establishing Your Own Private Foundation (a marketing system) (1998)
Prince, File Building Your Business: Marketing Your Way to a $100 Million Investment Advisory Business (1997) out of print

Published by Institutional Investor (212-224-3800)
Prince Private Wealth: Insights Into the High-Net-Worth Market (1999)
Prince, File Cultivating the Affluent II: Leveraging High-Net-Worth Client and Advisor Relationships (1997)
Prince, File Cultivating the Affluent: How to Segment and Serve the High-Net-Worth Market (1995)

Published by National Underwriter (800-543-0874)
Prince, Rathbun, Steiner The Charitable Giving Handbook (1997)
Prince, File Marketing Through Advisors: A Toolkit for Life Insurance Professionals (1996)
Prince, File Building an Affluent Clientele: Marketing Personal Lines Insurance to the Wealthy (1996)
Prince, File Marketing to the Affluent: A Toolkit for Life Insurance Professionals (1995)
Prince, File Marketing to Family Business Owners: A Toolkit for Life Insurance Professionals (1995)

Published by Jossey-Bass (888-378-2437)
Prince, File Seven Faces of Philanthropy (1994)

Published by Lexington House (800-356-5936)
Prince, McBride, File The Charitable Estate Planning Process: How to Find and Work with the Philanthropic Affluent (1994)

Published by PMIC (800-633-7467)
Prince, Phillips, Apolinsky Physician Financial Planning in a Changing Environment (1996)

To Jerry,

Yesterday & Today

- Russ Alan Prince

To Joe, Charlie and Mike

- Karen Maru File

Table of Contents

Preface

We have two parts to what we do. We do research and we do consulting.

For many years, a substantial portion of our professional time has been spent conducting research on the affluent market. We research just one thing, and try to do it very well. What we do is research the high-net-worth buyers of financial products and services and the small and mid-sized institutions they control (e.g., family offices, privately controlled firms, professional practices, endowments and foundations). A lot of that research found its way into this book.

We think research is useless unless it translates into action. Unless research on the affluent yields insights that investment advisors can use to become more profitable, it isn't useful. In order to insure that the insights from the research actually work, we are also consultants.

The core of our consulting practice is working with elite financial advisors and advisors who want to "fast track" to elite status. We pride ourselves on our track record of helping some of the top financial advisors in the business become even more successful. Every idea in here has been tested and re-tested by advisors. The processes and methods described here took years to learn, and were learned the hard way - in the field.

Because of the nature of Prince & Associates LLC we are quite limited with respect to the number of financial advisor clients we can deal with. This has led to the development of the High-Net-Worth Psychology Advanced Workshop and to this book.

We are confident that the approach of high-net-worth psychology, as well as the strategies and tactics detailed in these pages, can significantly enhance your investment advisory practice.

Russ Alan Prince

Karen Maru File

Connecticut

June, 1999

Forward

Marketing in the investment management industry today is as evolved as it has ever been. We started with techniques from Marketing 101 which were basic, formulaic and logical. And collectively, we've tried everything—from product benefit marketing to needs-based marketing to client-centered marketing to market segmentation by every possible variable to database mining to one-to-one marketing to value-added marketing to consultative marketing to cyber marketing. And here we are...successful, profitable, still seeking more explosive response and still aiming for higher targets.

Despite the many forms that marketing has taken, Russ Prince and Karen File have continued to push the very definition of marketing with their groundbreaking work in investor psychology.

Not only has their work helped marketing move beyond the superficial to the very core of an investor's psyche, it has linked psychological motivations to communications techniques, and ultimately, individual investment products.

On behalf of Prudential Investments, I selected the work of Prince & Associates as the basis for programs we have and will continue to develop to forge better, stronger and more meaningful relationships with all types of financial professionals. The results are a testimony to the accuracy and intuition of the research and analysis done by Russ and Karen, and its relevance to this industry.

High-Net-Worth Psychology: Finding, Winning and Keeping Affluent Investors is not just for financial services professionals and marketers—anyone who interacts with individual consumers for a living needs something from this book.

Good luck and good marketing!

Hannah Shaw Grove

Vice President

Prudential Investments

Introduction

In High-Net-Worth Psychology: Finding, Winning and Keeping Affluent Investors, Russ Alan Prince and Karen Maru File have delivered a landmark achievement in the financial services industry developing the first publication of its kind. The old saw that "everyone talks about the weather, but nobody does anything about it" has sadly been resonant of marketing to the affluent. As financial services providers know, affluent individuals are the lifeblood of this industry. Yet remarkably, there has not been a quantitatively-based, clear, systematic methodology to build an advisory business with the affluent.

Until now, that is.

True, there have been may books with exciting titles that touch on the periphery of the issue and share motivational anecdotes. But none have dealt with the crux of the matter, "How do I develop an affluent clientele and dramatically grow my business?" The conspicuous absence of such material has finally been filled by High-Net-Worth Psychology: Finding, Winning and Keeping Affluent Investors. This book is the Rosetta Stone of marketing to the affluent (of how to find, win, and keep affluent clients) providing a clear, logical model to follow for the advisor who is committed to entering the elite realm. Prince and File have done extensive research with hundreds of affluent individuals and numerous financial advisors, and quantitatively sifted the information to reveal and understand the techniques and practices used by elite financial advisors. But they did not stop there, they then converted it into a clear, systematic model that can be learned and used by anyone committed to improving their advisory business. For too long, financial advisors were left to trial and error to learn what worked best with affluent clients.

This not only takes many years to learn and perfect on one's own, but can also be extremely costly in lost opportunities, lost clients and lost profits. In High-Net-Worth Psychology, Prince and File have removed the trial and error. They have discovered what works. They have observed the best in the business and given you a clear, intelligible model to follow. As you read this book, you will see yourself in many of the techniques provided. You will get flashes of insight on why you lost one client, and won another. Your gut instinct will tell you the things you are learning are true. But most importantly, you will be able to hone the winning practices you are doing on an occasional basis to the point where they are second nature, seamless and successful.

Earlier I said this book was the Rosetta Stone of success with affluent clients, and it is. However, it is not a Holy Grail. What I mean by this comparison is it provides the advisor the necessary information to succeed, not succeed itself. To have success, a financial advisor will need to study these concepts, learn these techniques and consistently implement them—only then will they enter the elite financial advisor realm.

Brett Van Bortel

Senior Manager

VanKampen Funds

I

Understanding the Wealthy

1

Worlds of Wealth

Wealth is concentrated among relatively few people in the United States. In fact, just 4% of U.S. households control about half of all the private assets. The other 96% of all the households in the country share the other half.

> ***"It is better to have a permanent income than to be fascinating."***
>
> ***- Oscar Wilde***

That being said, which half of investors would you rather have as clients? Of course, it would be the wealthy people. In other words, it would be the 4% who control half of all the private wealth in the U.S. At the same time, from the remaining 96% you can still skim the cream of the crop—those who have more of the investable assets who sit atop this sector.

If you market investment and financial advisory services to the wealthy, your life will be easier, and your business will be much more profitable.

Who has Wealth?

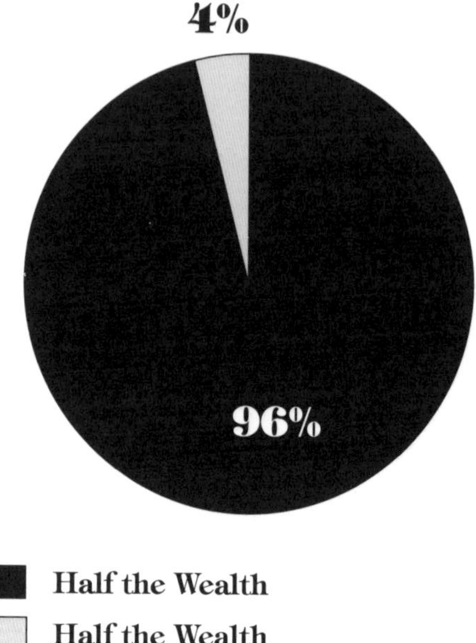

Why market to the wealthy? Here are a few reasons:

- Market to the wealthy and you will have fewer clients to cultivate and be concerned about.
- Market to the wealthy and you can build your business by working more with current clients instead of constantly trying to find new ones (do mining instead of prospecting).
- Market to the wealthy and your satisfied clients will prospect for you.

Why do investment advisors target the high-net-worth market?

Because that's where the money is.

- So let's focus on the moneyed class. Who are these 4%?
- How wealthy are they?
- How can you find them?

- What products and services do they buy?
- Why do they buy financial services in the way they do?

And, above all, how can you target and market to them successfully? All of these questions will be answered in the following pages.

For starters, the 4% and the high-end of the 96% have a minimum of $1 million in investable assets. While $1 million does not represent the enormous wealth it did in past decades, the threshold for being in the moneyed class (and in our target market) is having $1 million in an investment portfolio. This amount often equates to having $3 million or more in an estate (say a $1.5 million home, a $300K boat, a $200K ski house and $1 million in investable assets).

Willie Sutton, England's most famous robber, was asked, "Why do you rob banks?" His answer: "Because that's where the money is."

Under $1 million in investable assets represents a client in the other 96%. While this sector may still contain great investment advisory clients, our optimal target market is liquid millionaires.

Though our target market is liquid millionaires, it is important for you to recognize that the strategies and tactics explained in this book are

appropriate for less well-to-do investors (e.g., those with $100,000 in investable assets). While we developed the models and approaches based on affluent investors, many investment advisors have put these concepts to work and significantly increased their effectiveness with less wealthy investment clients. Still, one of the objectives of this book is to show you how you can move upscale. The place to start is to see how many wealthy investors there are.

How Much Wealth is There?

According to a *Merrill Lynch/Gemini Consulting* study, World Wealth Report 1998, there are $17.4 trillion in assets worldwide in the hands of high-net-worth investors (those having $1 million or more in investable assets). For global fee-based investment advisors, this represents an annuity revenue stream of close to $200 billion.

In North America, the same study estimates that there are $4.7 trillion in the hands of wealthy investors. Even with the market volatility in 1998, and especially during volatile markets in general, wealthy investors are where the money is (see Chapter 17).

These figures do not represent adequately the complete picture of the amount of money and consequently investable assets in the hands of the affluent. For example, consider one of the booming areas for investment advisors, the IRA rollover market. The multi-million dollar accounts that are set up as people retire prove to be an exceedingly attractive (and lucrative) pool of money searching for professional advice.

Another example of one of the many opportunities available to create and manage pools of assets is the field of charitable planning. Through the use of certain charitable trusts, for instance, you can help a wealthy donor easily and tax-effectively convert non-liquid assets such as real estate into liquid assets requiring investment expertise.

In general, the amount of wealth in search of high-quality investment advice is considerable. And, as we'll see in the next section, this amount is growing.

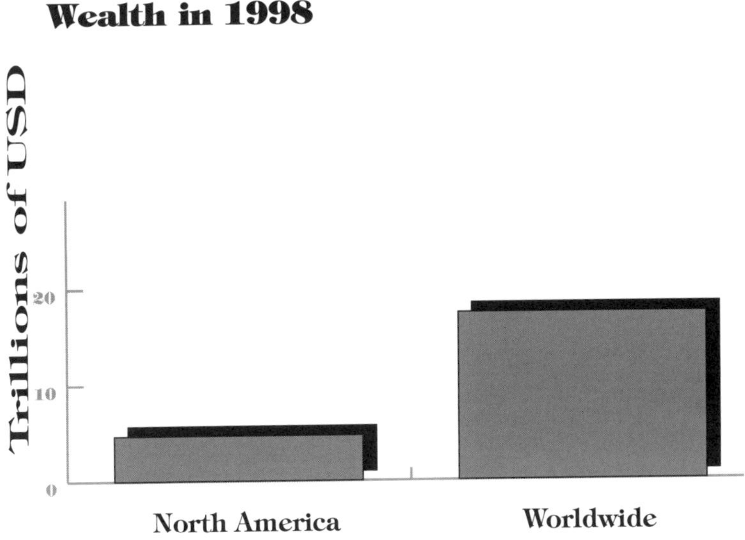

The Rich Are Getting Richer

Not only is there a great deal of money that can be professionally managed, but the assets controlled by the most affluent segment are

growing. In terms of global wealth, the total investable assets of high-net-worth investors is projected to rise to $23.1 trillion by the year 2000. The same is true in North America where the Merrill Lynch/Gemini Consulting study forecasts growth in assets owned by the upscale market will grow to about $5.8 trillion by the year 2000.

According to this study, the private portfolio market is growing 8% per year. Overall, wealth is growing six to 10 times as fast as is the number of households.

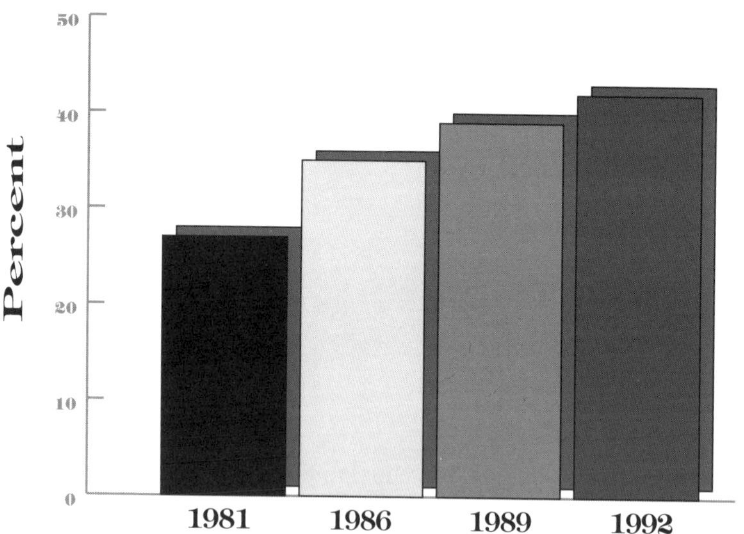

Once again, we're not even counting all the non-liquid assets that are being reconfigured into investable assets. By adding these assets the private portfolio market is growing at least 11% per year.

Not only do the rich control most of the assets, but they are getting richer. The top 1% of the richest families controlled 27% of all the private wealth in 1981, according to research by Edward Wolff of New York University. That proportion climbed to 35% in 1986, and to 39% in 1989. By the beginning of the 1990s, that percentage was up to 42%.

How The Rich Get Rich

In general, the wealthy generate their own wealth. Three-quarters of all affluent people made their money by owning a private business (64%) or a professional practice (13%). Few became wealthy by inheriting their money from their parents or through life insurance on a spouse (7%). Fewer yet became wealthy by working for a corporation (6%). One in 10 became wealthy from investments (10%). People become wealthy because of the businesses they own, as the figure on the following page shows.

According to the Small Business Administration, there are approximately 23.3 million non-farm businesses in the U.S., of which 99% are small. The SBA defines small as having 500 or fewer employees. These privately held businesses employ 53% of the private workforce, contribute 47% of all sales in the country and are responsible for 51% of the private gross domestic product.

How They Got Wealthy

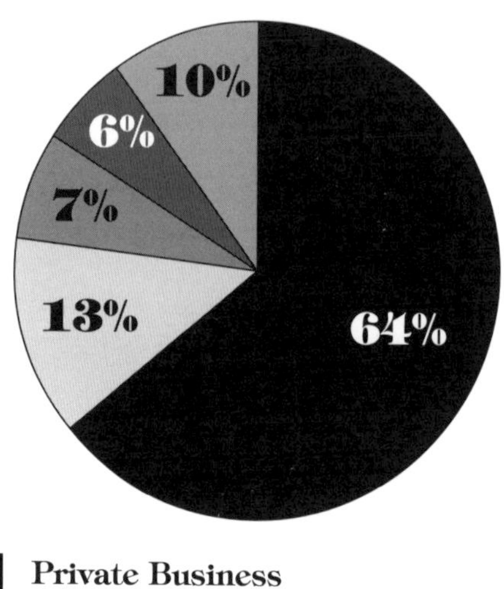

Private Business
Professional Practice
Inheritance
Corporate Employee
Investments

New business formation has been growing at about 3% per year recently, making the U.S. a hotbed of entrepreneurship. Smaller, privately held businesses power the economy and are the leading force in job creation. Throughout the world, the number one way to become wealthy is to own a successful business. These businesses spearhead innovation. Most importantly for investment advisors, these privately held businesses create significant private wealth.

There are other paths to wealth in the business world as well. In the second half of the twentieth century, many businesspeople also became wealthy with initial public offerings of stock. Distribution of stock options is also on the rise. Add the fact that retirement plan distributions will create a great many liquid millionaires and you'll want to watch all these opportunities. While privately held businesses are the number one route to private wealth, for some investment advisors, these other opportunities can be just as profitable.

Additional Investment Advisory Opportunities

If you focus solely on individual or personal investment advisory opportunities, you may inadvertently neglect additional significant business opportunities. As was just discussed, most affluent investors created their wealth by owning a privately held business. Other opportunities for managing assets in these firms include retirement plans, deferred compensation plans and cash management services.

In addition, affluent investors are well-networked and you in turn can leverage their networks. Through their personal and professional relationships, the affluent have significant influence in the investment management decisions of numerous institutions.

Finally, another area — and a burgeoning one — you can tap when you are well-networked with the affluent is the endowment and foundation market. The smaller charitable institutions in particular are in great need of high-quality investment advisor services.

Money on the Move

One of the biggest opportunities ever will occur over the next 50 years. During this time, the highly successful World War II generation will pass away and their assets will flow to their children. Cornell University economists Robert Avery and Michael S. Rendell project this transfer to be $10.4 trillion. Let's put this number into perspective; $10.4 trillion is equal to *twice* the country's gross national product.

"The thing about the Du Ponts is that some are very rich and others are just plain old rich."
—Pierre Samuel DuPont II

However, a word of caution is necessary. These assets are not all liquid assets instantly available for new money managers to chase. These assets include primary and secondary residences, operating businesses, tangible assets, real estate and other illiquid assets (at least initially illiquid). However, this transfer of wealth will result in new opportunities. Heirs almost always seek out new investment advisors, providing you with an opportunity to bring in new assets for management.

The Profitability of the Wealthy

Admittedly, closing a new affluent investor client can be costly and drawn out for an investment advisor. It may take months to bring in the first assets under management. However, even if we assume a "revenue-neutral" first year, the profitability of the client takes off in year two and thereafter. Affluent clients are highly profitable and you have the opportunity to increase your revenues from each affluent investor. According to most investment advisors, the recurring nature of the private wealth management business is one of its most attractive qualities.

To understand the comparative profitability of the affluent market, let's consider the investment management business. There are basically three types of client—retail, institutional and affluent. Of these three, it is only the affluent clients who are *relatively insensitive* to the cost of investment management advisory services. At the same time, affluent clients are *relatively insensitive* to poor investment performance for extended periods of time.

The Attractiveness of the Affluent Investor

Factors	Retail Investor	Institutional Investor	Affluent Investor
Price Sensitivity	Moderate	High	Low
Performance Sensitivity	High	Moderate-High	Low

Such is not the case with the retail investor who is highly sensitive to investment performance issues and is moderately attuned to pricing issues. Nor is it the case with institutional investors who are highly sensitive to pricing considerations and are moderately to highly sensitive to investment performance. Given these sensitivities, which type of client would *you* want? The wealthy are here to stay. Through both economic booms and severe depressions, there will always be a moneyed class. While the number of the wealthy grows and recedes with changes in the economy, the economic elite have always been with us. The affluent always have looked to professionals advisors to assist them in managing their financial affairs and this will not change.

The reason the affluent market has always been attractive to investment advisors is that it is the most *consistently profitable* market for financial services. The affluent market is expanding at a prodigious rate. While other investment management markets are flat or even contracting, the number of wealthy individuals in search of investment advisory services is growing, and growing quickly.

In addition to size and growth, there are other reasons for targeting the wealthy. Affluent investors represent an annuity business. In no other market can you find the type of client loyalty as with the wealthy. By providing quality investment services and products as well as skilled application of relationship management strategies, each of your affluent investor clients will represent a consistent revenue stream for you.

Why You Should Use High-Net-Worth Psychology

The private wealth industry is highly fragmented because of low barriers to entry. A personal or professional relationship with a wealthy investor is really all you need to get into the business. The continual relationship nature of the business translates into the ability of *almost* any investment advisor to make a living no matter the extent of the perceived competition. However, the real issue is how you define "make a living."

> ***"Money is a privilege to act as you will, and also a prohibition against doing as you please."***
> ***- Moses Goldman***

For some, making a living means getting by. On the other hand, for nearly all the investment advisors with whom we have studied and worked, make a living means a great deal more. It usually means becoming wealthy themselves. High-net-worth psychology can be very effective in helping you reach the top ranks of the investment advisory industry.

Now, how are you going to make it to the top in a fragmented, competitive field? How will you leverage client relationships to create an increasingly affluent client base? The most effective way we have found is by using high-net-worth psychology. Investment advisors who have worked with us and who use high-net-worth psychology report results such as the following:

- The ability to reduce the sales cycle by at least 40%;
- The ability to create 27% additional fee-based revenue annually; and
- The ability to produce 3 times the number of affluent client referrals.

For these investment advisors, there is another—and for many of them a more important—benefit of using high-net-worth psychology. What is more important than significantly building their investment advisory businesses? The answer is doing the best job possible for their clients.

Investment advisors who have adopted high-net-worth psychology are able to do a significantly better job helping their clients achieve their financial agendas. These investment advisors are doing a better job by being more adept at identifying what is really important to their clients, by being more proficient at communicating with them and by being more capable of providing the quality relationship clients want.

This is to say neither that investment advisors who have adopted high-net-worth psychology were not previously successful nor that they weren't doing a good job for their wealthy clients before they began applying high-net-worth psychology. What we've found is that high-net-worth psychology enabled these advisors to work more efficiently and effectively and, most of all, systematically.

Before continuing with the effectiveness of high-net-worth psychology let's look at its development.

A Brief Look Back

In 1994, *Institutional Investor* launched a newsletter entitled *Private Asset Management.* The audience for the newsletter was, and is, financial institutions and individual investment advisors targeting the wealthy investor. One of the features of the newsletter was research on the private wealth industry. In particular, the newsletter explored the investment behavior of the wealthy.

Prince & Associates LLC was commissioned to conduct the research on behalf of *Private Asset Management* because of our many years of experience researching the financial and philanthropic behavior of the affluent. In conjunction with *Institutional Investor/Private Asset Management,* we moved way up the knowledge curve concerning the psychology of the wealthy investor.

Based on the research conducted for *Institutional Investor/Private Asset Management,* we produced three research reports which were published in book form (see book list). A central component of the research was the psychographic segmentation of the affluent investor—high-net-worth psychology.

Not only have some of the most successful and prestigious private banks, private client groups of investment and commercial banks, brokerage firms, family offices, insurance companies and professional services firms gravitated to high-net-worth psychology, so too have many leading individual investment advisors.

In our consulting practice we work extensively with elite financial advisors around the world. With these elite financial advisors we have been able to develop more and more ways to use high-net-worth psychology effectively in client-facing situations. That's what it's all about, the ability to improve client-facing effectiveness. That means high-net-worth psychology has to work in the real world, and it does.

In reality, it has been these elite financial advisors who have shown us how to take the research and transform the findings into strategies and tactics that get bottom-line results. These advisors continue to help us refine the numerous applications of high-net-worth psychology.

Why would investment advisors responsible for hundreds of millions or billions of dollars be interested in high-net-worth psychology? Why would individual life insurance producers writing as much as $50 million or more in new premiums per year be interested in high-net-worth psychology? The answer is that it makes them more effective and efficient. It enables them to better leverage what they already do well. It helps them at the edges and it is the nuances that often make the difference. Users say the primary benefit is that high-net-worth enables them to take a more systematic approach.

A Systematic Approach

Not all affluent investors are alike. Still, if you're like most investment advisors, you have a canned way in which you approach a wealthy investor and in which you explain your services such as asset allocation. Sometimes you may customize your approach, but, as one investment advisor put it, "I usually go on automatic." Why do investment advisors sometimes "go on automatic?" Time pressure usually is the answer and it affects just about everyone.

In our research we find that even the best investment advisors fail to properly customize their approaches to wealthy investors. Furthermore, even among the elite financial advisors to whom we consult, we have found that, all too often, they stray from the way they know they should work. They periodically revert to bad habits including packaged presentations.

One of the most dramatic results of adopting high-net-worth psychology has been that investment advisors have been able to more systematically—and therefore consistently—meet the needs and wants of wealthy investors. Once again, we're not saying that before they started applying high-net-worth psychology investment advisors were not focused on the needs and wants of wealthy investors. However, when they began using the approach, for the most part, they became much more consistent.

Not only have we found that high-net-worth psychology works for investment advisors wanting to fast track to the elite levels, but it has also proven effective with those at the elite ranks. These high-end financial advisors apply the principles of high-net-worth psychology almost intuitively. For them, mastering the approach has made them much more consistent, which has translated into more business and more satisfied wealthy clients.

Both our experience and research findings reveal that high-net-worth psychology is effective in ensuring you carry out your work well and appropriately. Demands on time might offer an explanation, but they're not an excuse for not doing the best job possible.

High-net-worth psychology becomes all the more important because some investment advisors don't have the background, experience and training to be successful with wealthy investors. This framework provides the tools and techniques that are essential to achieve success in finding, winning and keeping affluent investors.

High-net-worth psychology originated in work done with *Institutional Investor's Private Asset Management* newsletter some years ago and since then it has been adopted by more and more leading investment advisors.

Their experience has enabled us to refine the concepts and techniques of using high-net-worth psychology. More than that, their experience has proven to us that high-net-worth psychology will shrink the sales cycle, increase client referrals, increase asset capture and render even the top advisors more consistent at what they do best. These are the reasons we wrote this book, and these are the reasons you should add high-net-worth psychology to your tool kit of professional skills.

"Social prosperity makes people happy, citizens free and the nation great."
- Victor Hugo

Who Are the Nine High-Net-Worth Personalities?

You have enough experience working with investors to know they're not all alike. This is especially true of the wealthy. You cannot treat all affluent clients the same. They accumulated their wealth in different ways, think about their wealth differently, and have different ideas about what their wealth represents. You need to consider these differences in the way you interact with them.

Granted, sometimes you don't have the time to create a customized strategy. One of these times is when you are prospecting. You don't know enough about the new prospect to represent yourself as effectively as you could. A new client may protect their privacy by being careful about what they tell you. You even can have a client for years and not really know them. What you need is a *system* for better understanding your prospect's or client's needs and wants.

> ***"We must resemble each other a little in order to understand each other, but we must be a little different to love each other."***
> ***- Paul Geraldy***

The best system for thinking about prospects and clients is to focus on their needs and wants — the benefits your

services and products provide in meeting their needs and wants.

First, you must determine what clients need and want. If you are like many investment advisors, you answer investment performance without blinking an eye.

Naturally, clients NEED and WANT solid investment performance. Achieving decent investment performance is why they come to you.

But, WHY do they need and want solid investment performance?

WHAT does money mean to them?

WHAT do they want to do with the money?

WHERE does their wealth fit in with how they envision life?

High-net-worth psychology answers those questions. For starters, high-net-worth psychology organizes wealthy individuals into groups based on WHY they invest — why they are interested in investment performance, why they pick the advisors they do. Knowing why allows you to focus directly on client needs and wants, leading to significantly greater client satisfaction. We find that:

- *High-net-worth psychology* overall is most effective in marketing and sales.
- *High-net-worth psychology* enables you to more effectively convert prospects into clients.
- *High-net-worth psychology* helps increase the retention rate of affluent clients, and the rate at which affluent clients refer others to you.
- *High-net-worth psychology* helps you to identify and benefit from asset capture opportunities.

What is high-net-worth psychology? It is a framework, a system, for understanding what wealthy people want from their investing, their investment relationships and from you as their investment advisor. This framework is a system of nine personality types.

High-Net-Worth Segments

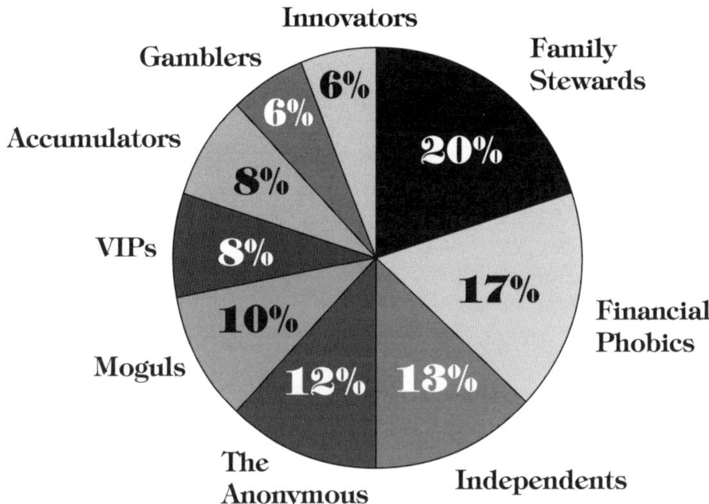

Let's explore the characteristics of each of the nine types of high-net-worth personalities. The following table shows the key needs, values and motivations for each personality. It shows what each wants from their investing program. It answers the question why each group wants good investment performance.

The 9 High-Net-Worth Personalities

FamilySteward	• Focus on investing to take care of their families. • Are conservative. • Are not very knowledgeable.
Financial PHOBICS	• Avoid focusing on investing. • Many have inherited the assets. • Are confused and frustrated by the responsibility of wealth.
Independents	• Exhibit drive for the type of personal freedom money makes possible. • Feel investing is a necessary means to an end. • Not interested in the process of investing.
theanonymous	• Confidentiality is their primary concern. • Prize privacy for their financial affairs. • Are likely to concentrate their assets and have few investment advisors.
Moguls	• Investing is another way of creating personal power. • Control is a primary concern. • Decisive.
VIPs	• Investing results in social recognition. • Prestige is important. • Like to affiliate with institutions and investment advisors with leading reputations.
ACCUMULATORS	• The only goal of investing is to make money. • Are investment performance oriented. • Are fairly knowledgeable and very involved.

GAMBLERS
- Relish the process of investing.
- Are very knowledgeable and involved.
- Have high risk tolerance.

INNOVATORS
- Are focused on leading-edge products and services.
- Are sophisticated; like complex products.
- Are technically savvy.

FamilyStewards

Investing IQ ★ ★ ★

"Good investing lets me take good care of my family."

The Family Steward invests in order to care for their family. Family Stewards often will have privately held businesses, and they like to have their children work in the business. When asked what their goals are for their investments, a typical Family Steward might say, "Good investing lets me take care of my family."

It is highly likely that many of your clients will be Family Stewards as they make up the largest group of affluent investors (20%). You probably already have Family Stewards among your client base. Think of your wealthier clients who have pictures of kids all around their offices, who have their children employed in their businesses, who live modestly yet have a significant asset pool and who are highly motivated to ensure their families are financially secure. How many Family Stewards come to mind?

Family Stewards are average in their knowledge of investing and personal finance. Their investing IQ is three out of five stars, five being the highest. The three stars for Family Stewards shows you they are middle-of-the-roaders when it comes to their financial sophistication. As you will see, there is another group that has only half a star because they are not at all knowledgeable. Conversely, a few high-net-worth personalities have five stars because they are very knowledgeable. According to this measure, Family Stewards are about average.

You must possess expertise to relate to Family Stewards. We'll see that many of the high-net-worth personalities want their investment advisors to be experts. The key to being an expert for a Family Steward is different than being an expert for an Innovator or for an Accumulator. For Family Stewards, expertise is about understanding which services you provide will enable them to best fulfill their perceived family obligations.

You also need to be careful and prudent to fit their investment philosophy. To accomplish this, you need to show that you are very protective of them and their goals. They need to feel that you understand them and their goals of protecting their family exceptionally well.

An investment advisor working with a Family Steward client might say, "There are a lot of ups and downs in the current market. Let's sit down to look at the situation and make sure your family is protected the way we want it to be."

Family Stewards are highly responsive to a variety of planning services because of their strong motivation to do the best by their families. They can readily understand why planning would put them in a better financial position.

According to our national research studies, 72% of Family Stewards are very interested in estate and financial planning, and 66% are very interested in asset allocation services.

Family Stewards are especially motivated when estate and financial planning services are positioned as ways through which they can help their families. For example, an advisor might suggest, "It's good you have decided to do an estate plan. In the plan I just finished, we were able to save on taxes so there was money to set aside for the grandchildren's education." Naturally everyone wants to save on taxes. The key point is that you tie the savings back to the dominant motivation behind their investing—their families.

Family Stewards are interested in a broad range of investment products that can help them meet their family goals. Among such products are managed accounts, private equity opportunities and funds of funds. The important element for Family Stewards is not the actual investment vehicle, it is the goal of safeguarding their families. The risk profile of a Family Steward tends to be conservative to moderate.

Family Steward Case Study

An investment advisor was introduced by one of his affluent clients to another wealthy individual who had a disabled daughter. From their first meeting, it was clear everything in that parent's life revolved around how he was going to protect his daughter Mary. The investment advisor quickly realized that this prospect was a Family Steward whose financial goals centered around the well-being of his daughter. They developed an appropriate portfolio and every time financial decisions were addressed, the investment advisor prefaced such decisions by saying, "Here is how this is going to help Mary..."

Shortly after the investment advisor constructed the portfolio, he began to receive unsolicited referrals from this client. These referrals were also wealthy people with children who had Muscular Dystrophy. As it turned out, his client belonged to an association for families with children who have this disability, and the client was so pleased with the detail and care taken on behalf of his child, he urged other parents to go to his investment advisor.

"He didn't have to climb the ladder. His family owned the ladder."

- Lawrence M. Apcar

Financial PHOBICS **Investing IQ**

"The last thing I want to talk about is investing money."

Financial Phobics are hard to miss. They would rather not learn anything about investing and they tend to be adamant about remaining financially unsophisticated. Instead of learning themselves, Financial Phobics would much rather delegate the management of their monies to a trusted investment advisor.

Financial Phobics are the least knowledgeable about money of any segment. They have a half a star to represent their Investment IQ, which is the lowest of all the high-net-worth personalities. We give them half a star because their financial sophistication generally ends after writing checks and using credit cards. They do not know anything about investments, and they know they don't know. They are looking for an investment advisor to take over the complete responsibility, but first they must feel they can trust the advisor.

This trait of passing the responsibility of investing to the advisor makes Financial Phobics a great group to have as clients. For one thing, they are the least sensitive to investment performance of any of the nine high-net-worth personalities. It's a big mistake to try and educate them about financial issues because if you do, they'll most likely walk away because that's not what they want. Instead, you always must work to build interpersonal trust.

To work successfully with Financial Phobics, they need to consider you a reliable and dedicated expert. Here, being an expert means you can take care of, or at least consult on, *all* their financial matters. They need to be able to count on your presence, your management of all the things they cannot bear to manage and your dedication to their best interests (because they generally can't look after them on their own.)

Because Financial Phobics do not want to understand investing, they will focus exclusively on their personal rapport with you, trying to determine whether or not they can trust you.

Financial Phobics are not interested in the various planning services. It is not that they don't need them—most do—but that they are not interested in participating in an extensive financial, estate, investment or tax planning process. The challenge for you is how to get them to commit to a process they need.

"If you can't stand the heat, get out of the kitchen."
- Harry S. Truman

An investment advisor working with a Financial Phobic might advise the following, "Many of my clients don't like to get bogged down in the details of a particular investment. Instead, they've learned they can trust my expertise to find them the best possible investments for their goals."

As you might have suspected by now, Financial Phobics are not interested in any particular financial products either. Though they need financial products they are not interested in them. They are not interested in learning about them and they are not interested in making decisions about them.

When a Financial Phobic wants to open an investment account, they are buying you and the comfort and trust they feel with you.

Financial Phobic Case Study

There is an investment advisory firm that has adopted catering to Financial Phobics as the core of their business. As the market steamed ahead during the mid-nineties at double-digit growth, the firm returned an average annual return of less than 5%.

In spite of these returns, the firm has not lost a single wealthy client. In fact, it grows its account base by more than 25% annually—all through new wealthy clients. Because of the firm's success in growing its account base, three years ago it instituted a $2 million minimum for new accounts.

This investment advisory firm is in Florida, and it targets widows. The money from the widows comes from life insurance, and whenever the advisors have a client meeting they talk about personal issues—Medicare, grandkids, golf. They touch on investments only briefly. In fact, this point is what accounts for their success with wealthy clients. The investment advisors focus, almost exclusively, on developing and enhancing personal rapport, not on the nuts-and-bolts of investing.

Independents

Investing IQ ★ ★ ★

"To me, successful investing means freedom."

Independents are an uncomplicated group. They just want to be free to do what they please. They actually may stay in a corporate job or run a business, but they absolutely need to know they could leave and bum around the world at any time. Knowing they could cut loose at any time is the liberating feeling Independents crave.

Independents have three stars for their Investment IQ and they are average in terms of their investment know-how. Therefore, Independents rely on their investment advisors for guidance, ideas and overall expertise.

To work effectively with Independents, you need to be the expert. Here, expert refers explicitly to your ability to provide investment advice that will enable them to do what they want. Independents want you to compensate for their own relative weakness and lack of investment expertise. However, they need constant reassurance that you are focused on the same goal of their investing as they are—financial independence. They will look to make sure that your recommendations and investment style fit with this goal.

In short, they want an expert that is going to get them out of that corporation at age 55. They are not focused on their families (like Family Stewards) and they do not center their decisions exclusively on interpersonal trust (like Financial Phobics). Their hot button is personal financial freedom via astute investing.

Several Independents have not done an adequate job of allocating assets. Consequently, they are interested in asset allocation services because they know they need their assets structured and invested properly. They are aware that asset allocation will help them achieve their goals. However, they don't necessarily want to know the specific investments (e.g., mutual funds) to which their money is headed. An investment advisor working with an Independent might approach the situation like, "I have put together asset allocation models for many people who have the goal of retiring early, and because I have a lot of experience in early retirement planning, I know what works best for your goal."

Another area of significant interest for the Independent is their interest in retirement distribution planning. Independents know that once they stop working, their money has to keep working as hard and as intelligently as possible. This is especially important to Independents because they are retiring early and will have a longer retirement. As such, retirement distribution planning creates another key issue for an investment advisor working with this personality.

Independents have broad investment interests. However, no specific financial product is especially interesting to a majority of

Independents, reflecting their relatively average knowledge of investing in general. Some are interested in private equity and others in managed accounts, although this could be because these are buzz word investments in affluent circles. Therefore, though Independents may express an interest in one of those products, an investment advisor would be wise to distinguish between clients' interests and their needs.

> ***"If we command our wealth, we shall be rich and free."***
> ***- Edmund Burke***

Independent Case Study

There was a chief engineer named John at an aerospace company. He had a 401(k) plan into which he had put money for many years. His company matched his contribution. There was also a profit sharing plan. John decided to look at his options and began talking with a couple of investment advisors.

One of them realized that John was an Independent. Acting on this insight, this investment advisor began every meeting with John by emphasizing that the key objective was to figure out the best way for John to take his distributions so that John would never have to worry about money again. The advisor convinced John that he understood his personal goals and the advisor was rewarded with a $3.2 million IRA rollover account.

the anonymous

Investing IQ ★ ★ ★ ★

"My money is my business and no one else's."

The Anonymous are a challenge to deal with until you truly understand their psychology. They are intensely private people, and do not want to disclose their financial positions to anyone. In order to work with an investment advisor, they need to feel absolutely confident that their privacy will be preserved.

Did you ever have a wealthy client that took forever to open up and feel comfortable with you? That wealthy client was probably one of the Anonymous. It will usually take some time before the Anonymous will provide you with a lot of information about themselves. The Anonymous feel that their money is their business and no one else's. This is an obvious hurdle for an investment advisor. However, once you win their trust, the Anonymous client will be loyal—in part because he or she does not want to talk to anyone else.

The Anonymous have solid personal expertise in investing. They come out at four stars which puts them above average among the nine high-net-worth personalities.

An interesting fact about the Anonymous is that they often come in by advisory referrals. In fact, when you receive an advisory referral you may want to consider that the affluent prospect might be one of the Anonymous. Can you guess why you'll never get a client referral from one of the Anonymous? Because they don't talk to each other, or to most anyone else, about financial matters.

In order to work effectively with the Anonymous, you should be extremely discrete and miss no opportunity to emphasize the lengths to which you will go to protect client information. Taking great care in handling their accounts is key as well. For example, every time you send them correspondence over which you have control you should stamp it confidential. You should also send it via a secure delivery service. Finally, always make sure you follow up with a phone call to confirm receipt of the package.

Because they are knowledgeable, the Anonymous want their investment advisors to have considerable expertise. Expertise refers to both investment proficiency and the ability to ensure confidentiality. Many of the Anonymous have not been through the basic planning processes of tax planning and estate planning because they are so tight-lipped about their holdings.

If you can secure the trust of the Anonymous, certain planning services are appropriate, in particular, tax planning and estate planning. A common theme with the Anonymous is anti-government sentiments. They dislike the government's knowledge of their financial dealings via tax returns, and want to pay lower taxes. An investment advisor working with the Anonymous might approach the subject like, "When it comes to your money, it's not what you earn, it's what you keep. Plus the less you have to report, the less the government or anyone else knows."

The Anonymous are attracted to investment products which enable them to preserve their privacy and/or protect their assets from taxation. Annuities fit this mold as they are attractive from a tax planning standpoint. Besides, they also avoid probate. Offshore accounts and sometimes precious metals are vehicles that hold investments privately. For any of these or similar products, you want to be sure to lead with the benefits of the product, that is, that the products will achieve the greater goals of privacy and lower taxes.

"What you see here,
What you do here, What you
hear here, When you leave here,
Let it stay here."
- Anonymous

Anonymous Case Study

Alex was referred to an investment advisor by his attorney. The investment advisor consulted initially by phone and set up a meeting. One of the first things Alex told the investment advisor was that he hated taxes. Alex also said he thought that the Internet made personal information too easy to access.

After a few questions, the investment advisor determined that Alex was one of the Anonymous. He told Alex he thought his concerns about privacy were justified and that confidentiality of all interactions was a priority. He then asked Alex where he would like to meet in the future in order to ensure privacy. Alex said he preferred his office. The investment advisor emphasized his security measures in all dealings with clients during the meeting and was rewarded with Alex's account.

Alex has been a client of this investment advisor for seven years and they meet infrequently. What's interesting is that they do not fax or use overnight delivery services. Whenever they need to exchange documents, they do so by messenger. Alex has rewarded his investment advisor with a 60% increase in assets over the initial account, totaling $6.8 million.

Moguls

Investing IQ ★ ★

"Being rich means power."

Moguls are motivated by power. Moguls seek control, influence and, yes, power in their families, business, community and investments. Look for certificates and credentials on the walls of their offices. Listen to hear if they drop names of powerful and influential people, though not necessarily famous people. Watch their interactions with others. Are they authoritarian or bossy? Are they direct? Very direct? If so, you may have a Mogul.

Moguls are not particularly knowledgeable about investing; for this they earn just two stars. However, Moguls may say they're knowledgeable about investing as investing is a way to create more sources of power. They are not interested in investing per se.

For you to successfully relate to Moguls, you have to acknowledge their power, and be powerful yourself. A Mogul does not want to work with a shrinking violet. However, Moguls want to be in ultimate control of the relationship. Moguls respond well to flattery and require authority over all investing decisions.

You need to emphasize ways in which Moguls have control over their financial affairs, in which they make the big decisions. You also need to be appropriately deferential. In making a presentation to a Mogul, an advisor needs to connect to their basic motivation, for example, "I've developed an asset allocation model that I'd like to present to you to get your approval. I need you to decide between a couple of alternatives."

Moguls find the idea of asset allocation very appealing because it means they can have control over their investments without having to be involved in day-to-day details. Moguls are big-picture people. As such, they are interested in asset protection services because they perceive themselves as important, prominent individuals who may be likely targets for lawsuits.

Moguls like products associated with power and with powerful people. They like access to exclusive products because they feel it is an acknowledgement of their power, which explains their affinity for hedge funds, private equity and funds of funds. All three of these products play to their desire for power and to be perceived as powerful.

"The only prize much cared for by the powerful is power. The prize of the general is not a bigger tent, but command."

- Oliver Wendell Holmes

Mogul Case Study

Bob was a partner in a very successful law firm. He and his wife had a daughter and son. A year ago, he had a stroke, but has fully recovered although he is still worried about his health. He is also worried about his family's financial well-being. His daughter continually maxes out her credit cards, just like her mother, whom he blames for this behavior. His son had a drug and alcohol abuse problem, and had never been good with money.

Bob felt he had no one that he could trust, and he felt he had to make sure his family did not fritter away all his money. He decided he needed to structure his estate so that his wife or kids wouldn't lead themselves into financial ruin after he was gone. He felt that he was the only one strong enough to do so.

His advisor was sensitive to Bob's psychology and control needs. He helped Bob structure an estate plan that addressed Bob's concerns and met his control needs.

VIPs

Investing IQ ★ ★ ★

"There are lots of ways to get respect and investing well is one of them."

VIPs are status oriented. They like prestige and the respect of others. Look around their offices for pictures of them with celebrities. These celebrities don't have to be nationally known figures, they may be famous only on a regional or local level. Observe luxurious furnishings and prestigious objects. Notice how positively they respond to your celebrity story, how they perk up with interest.

VIPs are not especially knowledgeable about investments. However, they might try to impress you with what they think is the right answer. In any case, they will ultimately rely on you as the investment expert.

To work successfully with a VIP, you will need to be particularly attentive and responsive. Applying appropriate deference is also useful. You should especially stress the reputation and prestige of your institution or firm and its association with famous people.

VIPs are not very interested in financial or estate plans as many already have them. Once you establish the general nature of these plans (and how recently they were established) you should advance the discussion to potential product. Down the road, you may find it appropriate to recommend that they review their plans, but do not push the issue too early in the relationship.

One of the VIPs' strongest interests lies in asset protection services because they can see themselves as minor celebrities who may need to insulate themselves from lawsuits. They are also interested in charitable giving because they see donations to various causes as a way to elevate their social standing.

"Authority does not work without prestige, Or prestige without distance."
- Charles DeGaulle

VIPs are especially attracted to investments that have an exclusive aura or cachet. Private equity is known to be difficult to enter, so VIPs like the chance to do so. Another enticing investment category is collectibles because they have the virtue of investment potential as well as ownership of a precious object or status symbol that can be displayed. As an investment advisor, you need to be respectful of this trait, being status conscious when working with them.

VIP Case Study

A wealthy client introduced a prospect named Victor to her investment advisor. The investment advisor used the high-net-worth psychology approach to determine that Victor was a VIP. In the course of several phone conversations it became clear that Victor already had a financial plan and used the services of a number of money managers. There was nothing really motivating him to open a new account with this investment advisor.

The investment advisor approached Victor with a plan to develop a private foundation in the client's name, and positioned it to appeal to the VIP profile. In other words, the investment advisor pitched the private foundation as "the way people of your stature give."

Victor became intrigued, especially after the investment advisor showed him certain tax advantages. After almost a year of discussion, Victor had become so pleased by the investment advisor's service that he transferred just shy of $3 million for discretionary management by this advisor. The lesson here is that you can use high-net-worth psychology to get a foot in the door which in the end may lead to greater assets under management.

ACCUMULATORS **Investing IQ ★ ★ ★ ★**

"You can never be too rich or too thin.

Thin doesn't matter, rich matters."

Accumulators are the most focused personality on investment performance of all the high-net-worth. For Accumulators, capital appreciation is an end in itself. They don't want the money to do anything; they just want the money to grow.

For all of their focus on accumulating assets, Accumulators are more knowledgeable than some high-net-worth personalities, but they are not the most savvy investors (as denoted by the four stars). Though you may have to educate Accumulators they will be interested in what you have to say and are motivated to learn more.

To work with an Accumulator, you have to continually repeat back to them what their goals and motivations are. They are performance driven, and expect you to be the same way—concentrating on piling up those assets and congratulating each other on successful performance results.

Accumulators are open to various planning services, especially if those services will result in more money. For many of the affluent, and especially for Accumulators, it's not how much you make, but how much you keep. That's why planning services like estate and tax planning are of keen interest. Asset allocation services are also attractive because the point of asset allocation is to maximize long-term results.

Financial planning results in more efficient and effective use of financial assets—an appealing means to an end for Accumulators. An investment advisor pitching to an Accumulator might want to emphasize that they do considerable planning for every client to minimize taxes, ensuring that the client's money will grow as quickly as possible.

Accumulators, more than many other high-net-worth personalities, have broad investment interests. Actually, they are interested in anything that will make them money and interested in whatever will bring them the best return for their risk level. Private equity and even collectibles sound appealing to some Accumulators because those are asset classes in which they are generally not yet investing.

"A man who has a million dollars is as well off as if he were rich."

- John Jacob Astor III

Accumulator Case Study

There was an investment advisor with a physician client who had an account worth over $5 million. The physician didn't care about protecting his family, saying, "Why should I leave it to them? They didn't work for it." He didn't care about power or yachts or freedom. All he cared about was watching his money grow, and he was consistently critical of his investment advisor.

The physician always was asking why the funds the investment advisor chose did not beat this or that fund. The investment advisor would reply that no one can pick the leading fund year after year. Then he would try to educate the doctor about investing and why returns fluctuated. Nevertheless, the doctor would become angry. The investment advisor realized he had an Accumulator on his hands.

With that HNW Psychology insight, he soon understood he was doing the wrong thing trying to educate his client on the nuts-and-bolts of investing. So instead, he began every meeting, conversation and sentence with, "This plan is what is going to give you the most money over our 10-year plan." By so doing he took the client's focus off year to year, and kept it on the long-term plan for maximizing gains. He also kept the client six years and counting.

GAMBLERS

Investing IQ ★ ★ ★ ★ ★

"You have better odds playing the market than at Vegas."

Gamblers are a stereotype. They love the excitement of the market—the drama of investing, the thrill of the big win. For Gamblers, investing is their hobby. For some it is their work, and for a few it is their life.

Gamblers are very knowledgeable though they are not always astute. Gamblers believe it is possible to consistently beat the market and they like to recount their big victories. Not surprisingly, they often have a higher than usual risk tolerance. They call frequently and take a lot of your time, but they tend to be active traders as well as long-term investors, applying a percentage of their portfolio to each strategy.

Gamblers love to find people with whom they can talk about investing and need their investment advisors to be as involved as they are. They also like their investment advisors to share in the emotional excitement of investing.

When it comes down to it, Gamblers want a playmate. They want you, as their investment advisors, to be as much of an expert as they are. They also want you to eat, breathe and sleep investing and the market. And, they want you to have an exciting style. They like their investment advisors to be plugged in and energetic.

Most Gamblers say they are not particularly interested in having someone approach them with planning services such as a financial plan unless it is truly state-of-the-art. For instance, consider sophisticated asset allocation modeling. Most asset allocation models deal only with investable assets. For Gamblers, you will need to deal with asset allocation models that incorporate all their assets such as life insurance, real estate and retirement assets.

Gamblers are interested in investment products such as hedge funds and derivatives because there is the possibility of big returns. They like the leverage and risk profile of these investment vehicles. It's their kind of style.

Gambler Case Study

For one investment advisor, the majority of his clients are Gamblers. Like his clients, his life is the market. His enthusiasm coupled with his knowledge make him ideal for working with Gamblers.

In meeting a wealthy prospect, it takes him less than five minutes to determine if the person is a Gambler, and if the prospect is a Gambler, then getting the business is a slam dunk. Why? Because the investment advisor and the wealthy prospect are immediately on the same wavelength. Rapport is instantaneous.

One of his clients with about $40 million under management—half in a managed account and the other half for trading—talks to him almost every day. Even when the client went on vacation, he called every day. Both of them relish the excitement of the markets and that's what makes the relationship work.

INNOVATORS **Investing IQ ★ ★ ★ ★ ★**

"Derivatives were the best thing to happen to investors."

Innovators, like Gamblers, are extremely knowledgeable investors. However, their orientation is a bit different. Innovators like to be at the cutting edge of the money management field. They like new products and services, and sophisticated analytical methods. Innovators often have technical backgrounds, and might be computer programmers, engineers or mathematicians.

Innovators are substantially above average in their investment expertise and they, like Gamblers, have five stars representing their investing knowledge. However, they are tightly focused on the latest thinking in the money management field.

For you to earn the trust, and assets, of an Innovator, you have to prove your own worth in terms of leading-edge product expertise. Innovators look to their advisors to keep them sharp. They also expect that you will be as up on modern portfolio theory as they are, and that you look forward as much as they do to opportunities to discuss. Bear in mind

> ***"The thing that makes a creative person is to be creative, and that is all there is to it."***
> ***- Edward Albee***

that it is not unusual for Innovators to be running sophisticated analytical software on their own.

Like Gamblers, Innovators are interested only in the most sophisticated planning services. If you are conducting an asset allocation analysis, you should be prepared to review with them the various assumptions built into the model with which you are working.

At the same time, Innovators are eager to take advantage of a number of interesting investment opportunities, including private equity and hedge funds. They are also generally fond of derivatives. These investments fit their passion for leading-edge products. In fact, some Innovators have been known to discuss the mathematics behind swap transactions with their investment advisors.

Innovator Case Study

Robert is a computer scientist who made millions designing industry specific enterprise software. In fact, his core software program is one of the most widely used packages of its kind. His software has made him extremely wealthy.

Robert is a self-proclaimed nerd. He is interested in the mathematics of money management and his primary investment advisor is similarly focused on the mathematics of money management. What is critical for the investment advisor is her ability to discuss everything from Sharpe ratios to the efficient frontier. In fact, every investment is dissected along these lines.

It took a long time for Robert to find an investment advisor who was sufficiently technically astute to keep up with him. Being as knowledgeable as he is, why does Robert need to employ the services of an investment advisor? First, he requires someone to help him think through the issues. Second, he needs someone to bring him the latest thinking in the field. Third, he needs someone tied into Wall Street who can implement his investment desires.

Working with Innovators requires a very high degree of technical sophistication. Those investment advisors who recognize affluent investors as Innovators and can keep them at the cutting edge will be greatly rewarded for their efforts.

To those who have been investment advisors for a while, these high-net-worth personalities are all too familiar. "Sure, I know people who fit all these types." For some, however, these personalities are not as intuitive. The table that follows provides an example as to how to position your services most effectively for each of the high-net-worth personalities.

> ***"In touching money we touch the keystone of character."***
> ***- John Ruskin***

High-Net-Worth Personalities	***Positioning Statement***
Family Steward	"You have worked hard to get to a place where you can take care of your family and insure their security. Now it's time to put a plan in place that will assure you that your family will be taken care of in just the way you want. It will be somewhat complicated—trusts and the like—but it will meet your goal of taking care of your family."
Financial Phobics	"Because you would rather spend your time with family and things important to you, you need a group of people who will handle your financial matters. We understand your need to trust people to take care of you as if you were their mother. This reminds me of Mrs. Brown..."

High-Net-Worth Personalities	***Positioning Statement***
Independents	"You have said the most important thing to you is having enough money so that you can do whatever you want. Financial independence is your goal. We have been very successful in helping people achieve this independence. The first step is to work on a plan together that will help you reach your goals..."
theanonymous	"One of the things we do very well here is protect our clients' privacy. The "private" in private banking is there for a reason. We take client confidentiality very seriously. Let me tell you some of what we do..."
Moguls	"We think it is extremely important for our clients to have complete control over their financial affairs. Our goal is to put you in a position of power so you can be efficient and decisive."
VIPs	"Let me show you our art advisory department. Many of our clients have significant and well-known art collections. We work suitably for the internationally famous because of our global presence..."
ACCUMULATORS	"You are performance oriented, and a straight-to-the-bottom-line investor. You will want to know about each money manager's performance. Let's go over the numbers."

High-Net-Worth Personalities (continued)	***Positioning Statement***
GAMBLERS	"Not everyone is able to tolerate the risk you do. It makes you a unique investor, but a kind we understand. We have some special opportunities for investors like yourself, who can lean out further than most..."
INNOVATORS	"Because you are interested in the cutting edge of investment technology, maintaining a relationship with us makes sense. You'll be interested in our new..."

High-net-worth personalities can be targeted for specific investment products and services. Estate and comprehensive financial planning are interesting to Family Stewards and Independents because of their penchant for the future. Charitable giving motivates VIPs because of their interest in prestige and status; affiliation with important charities can bring them both of these things.

Business succession is important to Family Stewards and Moguls; the former because of their need to take care of their families (many of whom typically work in the business) and the latter because it is a way of continuing control over others. Asset protection is interesting to the Anonymous because of the additional layers of privacy it offers. Innovators like asset protection for a different reason, because it is new.

Retirement plans interest many of the nine high-net-worth personalities, but especially Family Stewards and Moguls. Corporate benefits are of central concern to Accumulators, who want to maximize their compensation.

Because Gamblers and Innovators are most likely to have a personal hand in managing a portion of their portfolios, brokerage services appeal to these personalities.

While some of the high-net-worth personalities might have a preference for certain types of financial services, it is still up to you to determine what is the best course of action when it comes to a particular client. It's like the investment management services you currently provide. You develop an investment portfolio for a client based on their needs, wants, risk levels, and the like. It's the appropriate investment portfolio for that client. By using high-net-worth psychology you are simply more effectively positioning that portfolio to the affluent investor.

Top Targets for Financial Services

Services	Top Personalities	Runner-up Personalities
Estate/Financial planning	Family Stewards	Independents
Charitable giving	VIPs	Moguls
Business succession	Family Stewards	Moguls
Asset protection/ Risk management	The Anonymous	VIPs
Retirement planning	Family Stewards	Moguls
Corporate benefits	Independents	Family Stewards
Investment management	Acculumators	Gamblers
Brokerage	Innovators	Gamblers

Family Steward? Financial Phobic? Profiling Clients the High-Net-Worth Psychology Way

So far, the high-net-worth psychology approach must make sense to you. That you are reading this book indicates you have sold enough investment advisory services and products to wealthy people to know they have distinctive patterns of thinking and acting. Now, you recognize the need to promote your investment advisory services differently based on with whom you are working. In addition, you understand that different types of high-net-worth investors will require you to manage relationships differently.

> *"The good thing about being rich is when you drop a Tic Tac, you don't have to pick it up—until nobody's looking."*
> *- John Kent Cooke*

As mentioned before, these are not new revelations. As a matter of fact, they are probably part and parcel of much of what you already do. Remember, the biggest benefit the elite financial advisors get out of using high-net-worth psychology is a way of doing what they do so well consistently. For many financial advisors, including the elite, high-net-worth psychology has been exceedingly effective in enabling them to better manage the nuances. It is these nuances that often make the difference when working with the very wealthy.

Who's Who

In working with many investment advisors, we have found that some are able to easily identify affluent investors as one of the nine high-net-worth personalities. How are they able to do this so easily? They do so because they are already segmenting their wealthy clients intuitively. Still, most of these investment advisors have become more proficient because high-net-worth psychology has enabled them to be much more systematic when working with affluent investors. And, as we discussed in Chapter 2, the real magic of high-net-worth psychology, for many top investment advisors, is that it creates consistency.

For advisors learning about the high-net-worth concept for the first time, it can seem like a challenge to discern a Family Steward from a VIP, or a Mogul from an Accumulator, or an Innovator from a Gambler from an Anonymous. As such, it would be helpful to have a reliable way to classify your clients and prospects by their high-net-worth personalities. This chapter describes how to make those assessments based on a natural way of interacting with your affluent clients. High-net-worth psychology is based on people's deepest values and motivations, so you can figure out who the investors are.

The experience of those investment advisors who have incorporated high-net-worth psychology into their practices has been that they can readily and accurately match the high-net-worth personality with the affluent investor. All it takes is a little practice. As with many new things, it might seem a little difficult in the beginning, but, rest assured, it becomes easy after a short period of time.

Notice What's Around You

To figure out who is who, begin with the environment.

You want your affluent clients or prospects to reveal their goals, dreams, wishes, wants and needs. You need this information to most effectively help them. Along the way, it is important to learn what they want in an investment advisor, how they like to be helped and who else they want to involve in the process (e.g., other professional advisors, family members, etc.).

Wealthy investors are most likely to share this kind of information with investment advisors if they are truly comfortable with advisors. In general, face-to-face meetings are the most comfortable for people as there is more time to talk, you can see the other person's expression and you can more easily ensure you are understood.

If possible, you should meet on the client's home turf — their home office, for example. You'll have the opportunity to read their environment, and their environment is a reflection of their personality.

Once you are at the affluent investor's home or office, take notice of the surroundings. Some investment advisors say they look for family photos as a clue to Family Stewards, whereas a clean desk might be a sign of an Anonymous. A wall of photos and awards could be a tip-off to a VIP. A huge office, imposing desk and several subordinates could mean a Mogul. Look for these kinds of signs and signals.

Their environments can give you a strong indication as to their high-net-worth personalities. You can confirm your impression later as you talk with your wealthy client or prospect.

In your initial meeting or meetings with a wealthy prospect, ask them questions. A good rule is 70% or more prospect talking, 30% or less you talking. If the wealthy prospect is the one doing most of the talking, you're getting the data you need. You're also beginning to build that all-important personal rapport.

In some situations, you're not going to have the option to spend most of the time asking questions and listening. Sometimes wealthy prospects want to hear what you have to say.

The 70% / 30% Rule

Think about your initial meetings with affluent prospects. Who is asking most of the questions? Who does most of the talking? Why?

We have observed that too many investment advisors spend too much time talking about themselves when it is unnecessary. For the most part, we've found that the affluent investor knows who you are and something about what you do. While it's often useful to provide a thumbnail sketch of yourself and your firm, you will usually end up better off letting the affluent prospect tell you their story.

Ask Opening and Follow-up Questions

When you ask questions, be sure they are open-ended or broad. Avoid questions a prospect can answer with simply "yes" or "no". "Yes" or "no" questions end a conversation quickly or they can make a conversation feel like an interrogation.

Furthermore, the best investment advisors look for extremes in the answers given by a wealthy prospect or client. For example, look for ways this person is really different from others regarding investment goals, motivations, values or financial interest. Then ask follow-up questions to confirm your ideas.

In the table below are a set of questions that will help you identify a client or prospect by their high-net-worth personality. You will recognize many of these questions and that is the point. The questions are supposed to be ones you would readily ask at a meeting. However, the key is not in the questions, it is in the answers.

To really dig down and understand affluent investors, you need to understand how they think and feel. The questions do not tell you this, rather the answers tell you how they think and feel. So, the key is in listening, and knowing what you are listening for. Each of the nine high-net-worth personalities will respond to the questions differently. Thus, what you're looking for is how they answer the questions.

As you are talking things over with the affluent prospect, it's often effective to start with the "opener questions". Depending on how the conversation progresses, you might want to follow-up with the questions in the right-hand column. By listening to the affluent investor's answers to these questions, you will be able to assign their high-net-worth personality. After talking with several prospects, you will be able to identify each wealthy investor's high-net-worth-personality.

You may need to ask only one or two of these questions, or you may need to ask most of them. Once you start using these questions, you'll find ways of asking these questions that work best for you. The key is that you pick up the unmistakable traits of each of the nine high-net-worth personalities as you talk back and forth with your clients.

Opener Questions	*Follow-up Questions*
What would you like your investments to achieve?	Is it to take care of your family or be financially independent?
When you think about your money, what concerns, needs or feelings come to mind?	**Are you more interested in accumulating it or in what it can do for you? And, what can money do for you?**
How involved do you like to be in the investing process?	Is investing something you like to do or have to do?
How important to you is confidentiality of your financial affairs?	**Is there anyone else who needs to be in the loop on our investment planning decisions?**

What would you like your investments to achieve? Is it to take care of your family or to be more financially independent?

This set of opener and follow-up questions will quickly let you identify two of the high-net-worth personalities—Family Stewards and Independents.

Family Stewards, you will recall, are affluent investors whose primary life motivation is to protect their families in every way possible, including financially. Family Stewards are often business owners, and tend to keep a lot of assets in the business so the enterprise can provide employment for many family members.

Family Stewards are very forward looking, and are as concerned about the education of grandchildren as helping children with down payments on their houses. So if you ask this question of Family Stewards, you will hear all about what they would like their money to do for their families.

Independents will answer this question at the other extreme. Independents are true to their name. They want personal independence. Independents dream about chucking it all and sailing off into the sunset. Their goal is to have their portfolios buy them personal autonomy which they value above all.

If you ask this question of an Independent, you will not hear much about their families. You will hear about a desired condo on the golf course, or about hiking in remote places or about other hobbies. However, listen carefully for themes of freedom and independence, not about material possessions like the set of golf clubs or the boat.

The other personalities will answer this question more or less in the middle. There will be some mention of the family, and a bit about the life they want to lead in retirement, but compared to the self-sacrificing Family Stewards and the self-fulfilling Independents, everyone else is pretty much middle of the road.

When you think about your money, what concerns, needs or feelings come to mind? Are you more interested in accumulating it or in what it can do for you? And, what can money do for you?

These questions will help you find Accumulators, Moguls and VIPs, and to tell the difference among them.

Accumulators are often smoked out by the key word, accumulate. They are more financially savvy than most of the other personalities. They are focused on just one goal—accumulating more assets. Accumulators are not particularly concerned with what can be done with the money; they are driven to accumulate it. Their answer will usually be something like, "I just want my portfolio to grow as quickly as possible."

Contrarily, Moguls and VIPs are interested in money because of what it can do for them. Moguls value money because it empowers them, and power is all-important to Moguls. They like to control the people and environments around them. In working with Moguls, it's important that you and others in the firm treat them with the kind of deference and respect you would grant to people of power. Moguls even are sensitive to the nuances of where people sit and how people are introduced. More money enables Moguls to have things more their way.

VIPs are status oriented. They like to be recognized and acknowledged and treasure prestigious surroundings and trophy possessions. They are interested in what money can do for them, but their examples will focus on material possessions — a wonderful new house, fabulous trips or a new sailboat. VIPs seek asset appreciation because of what it can buy and the life style it can confer.

How involved do you like to be in the investing process? Is investing something you like to do or have to do?

These questions are extremely effective in identifying the Financial Phobics, Gamblers and Innovators.

Financial Phobics dislike investing. They are scared of it and highly intimidated. When you ask them a question like the above, you will hear a lot about how much they do not like investing, and how they are burdened by it being something they have to do or worry about. Or they could go another route — quickly change the subject.

Ask this question of a Gambler or an Innovator, and you will hear enthusiasm and commitment. They like, even love, investing. Gamblers and Innovators are by far the most knowledgeable and expert of all the personalities.

Listen closely to tell the difference between the Gambler and the Innovator. Gamblers live and breathe investing. It is their hobby and often their life. Gamblers love the thrill of market volatility.

Innovators are also extremely knowledgeable, though technically so. They like to be at the frontier of investment approaches, the cutting edge. They are enthralled not by the thrill of investing, but by being at the forefront of money management.

How important to you is confidentiality of your financial affairs? Is there anyone else who needs to be in the loop on our investment planning decisions?

This question is designed to identify one particular group — the Anonymous.

Remember, we're focused on how they say something as well as

what they say. Obviously, not too many affluent investors will say that confidentiality is unimportant. However, the Anonymous are fervent about it. They will explain how central this concern is to them, and how essential it is in any advisory relationship.

The Anonymous are fearful and worried about personal security and confidentiality. They need constant assurance that you are protecting the integrity of their information as well as their investments. They are average in their understanding of investments.

As you can see, there isn't much of a secret to the technique for any of the nine personalities. Asking questions about your wealthy prospect's or client's wants and needs is what you do anyway. You probably already ask questions a lot like these. High-net-worth psychology just gives you something new to listen for in their answers so you can serve them better.

Float Trial Balloons

Okay, you have arrived at the stage where you think you know what personality type a client is, but you want to make absolutely sure. How can you do that? Float a trial balloon — it allows you to confirm or disprove your hunch, or try another tack if you have missed the mark.

Floating a trial balloon is relatively easy. Simply follow the process in this flow-chart.

Trial Balloon Ideas —Creating and Floating Trial Balloon Ideas

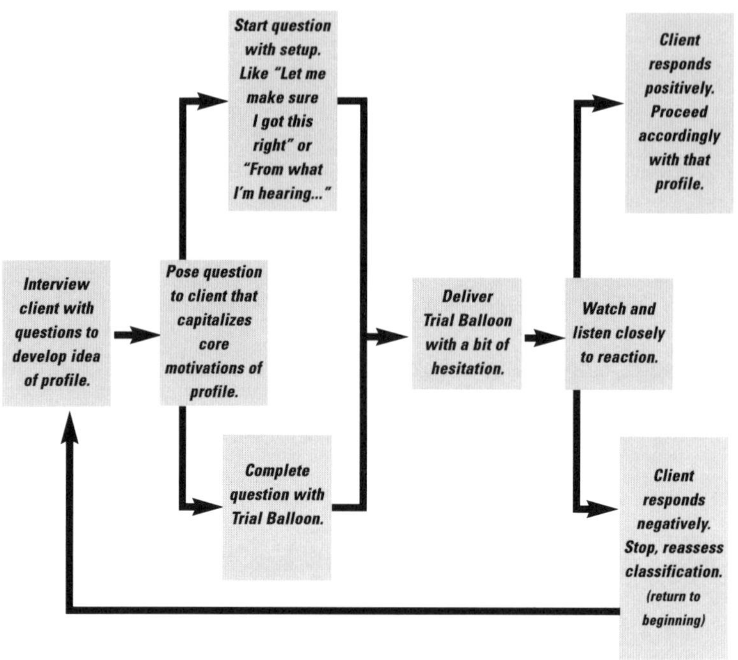

In this example, you thought someone might be an Accumulator. So you came up with the following trial balloon question, "After having a chance to get to know you, it seems that you are very astute about money. You know how to save it and how to make it grow. You don't spend it frivolously on material things. The most important thing to you is to grow those assets. Do I have that right?"

If they say yes, you have confirmed that they are an Accumulator. If they seem uncomfortable or hesitant, drop back and reassess your classification of their personality.

High-Net-Worth Personalities	***Sample Trail Balloons***
Family Steward	"...It seems your family's well-being is your primary concern. The most important thing is to protect the family. Do I have that right?"
Financial Phobics	"...From what you have said, it sounds as though managing money and making investment decisions is confusing and frustrating for you. Is that right?"
Independents	"...You seem to be the type of person who is absolutely focused on being financially independent, so you are free to do whatever you want. Is that true?"
the anonymous	"...I think keeping a client's affairs absolutely confidential is one of the most important services an advisor can provide a client. It seems that privacy is of paramount importance to you. Do I have that right?"
Moguls	"...I can see that you are as successful as you are because you insist on personal control over your affairs. In any investment advisory relationship, you will want power over all decisions and ultimate control, is this right?"
VIPs	"...You were interested when I was talking about some of the celebrities and well-known people who use our firm. It's important to me to affiliate with these sorts of people, and it is to you, too, isn't it?"

High-Net-Worth Personalities	*Sample Trail Balloons (continued)*
Accumulators	"... After having a chance to get to know you, it seems that you are very astute about money. You know how to save it and how to make it grow. You don't spend it frivolously on material things. The most important thing to you is to grow those assets. Do I have that right?
Gamblers	"...It looks to me like investing is very exciting for you—one of your favorite things to do. Isn't that so?"
Innovators	"...From what we've said, it seems that you are one of the very few very sophisticated investors. It sounds like one of the most important things for you is to work with a firm that can keep you at the cutting edge. Is this right?"

Do's and Don'ts

As you develop your skills in identifying the high-net-worth psychology of your affluent clients, keep these things to do and don't do in mind.

DO	DON'T
Notice what is around you; keep a mental checklist of observable items in the surroundings	Get technical
70% listening, 30% talking	Do all the talking
Use opening and follow-up questions carefully	Make assumptions about what clients want
Test your classification with a trial balloon	Become too rigid about the nine types

Do listen carefully as the affluent investor answers the opening and follow-up questions. Watch for what they respond to and what interests them. See what makes them open up.

Do make a mental checklist of items you see around you. Watch their behavior. See if you can figure out what they value. Do they have pictures around the office? If so, what are these pictures of?

Keep the client talking with open-ended questions so you get most of the information. Finally, test your classification with a trial balloon.

At the same time, there are some don'ts to keep in mind as well. Don't get technical unless you are talking to a Gambler or an Innovator—it will just turn off the personalities. Don't do all the talking. And, don't make assumptions about what clients want, even using the high-net-worth psychology approach. Get clients to tell you.

Test Your High-Net-Worth IQ With These Affluent Investor Situations

Investment advisors who we have trained in using the system say it becomes second nature very quickly. They say it takes a little effort to learn all the personalities, but after trying it out on their current clients, they are able to easily classify prospects.

Occasionally, a prospect or client will appear to be a combination, but most affluent investors have a single, dominant high-net-worth personality and that's the one in which you are most interested. Why? Because that's the "core logic" behind how the majority of the monies are to be managed.

Try your hand at the following situations. The answers are at the end of the chapter.

Client 1

You meet with Tom Anders at a party the evening after a major correction on Wall Street. While you are talking with him about the market, he tells you he's less than overwhelmed with the performance of his investment portfolio and wants to hear what you will do for him, so you set up a meeting.

His office is in a nondescript building and his office has a linoleum floor and an older desk and chairs. There are no plants or pictures. You know Tom is wealthy, and you are a little surprised by his environment.

You start by explaining the more you were to know about his investment goals, the more you could help him. You ask, "What would you like your investing to achieve?" Tom Anders pauses. "Well, you could say I just want it to achieve what it should, which is to appreciate."

You decide to try the second question. "When it comes to letting your money appreciate, what needs or concerns come to mind?" He is quicker to respond this time. "Well, I guess it's not getting the performance I was expecting." You go back to the first follow-up. "Is what you are trying to achieve taking care of your family, or being financially independent or growing your assets?" "Well, put that way, I guess you'd have to say growing the assets."

What high-net-worth personality is Tom Anders?

- ❑ FamilySteward
- ❑ **Financial PHOBIC**
- ❑ **Independent**
- ❑ **the**anonymous
- ❑ ***Mogul***
- ❑ VIP
- ❑ ACCUMULATOR
- ❑ GAMBLER
- ❑ INNOVATOR

Client 2

You are referred to Frederick Ford by one of your clients. He agrees to meet with you when you call. Before getting off the phone, he asks you if your firm does hedge funds. He meets you in his home office. A computer with Bloomberg sits on his desk.

He immediately asks you about the merger that has just been announced. You talk about that for a few minutes and then ask him, "Let's step back a moment. What would you like your investments to achieve?"

He talks about rate of return and issues in portfolio performance measurement. You follow up with, "So what's important to you when you think about your investing?" He talks about style drift. You move on to, "So how involved do you like to be in the investing process?" He points to the screen, "Completely involved. I do some of my own trading, and I work with several advisors, but very closely."

"What about investing and trading interests you so much?" you ask. "Well, it is a wild ride. It's changing all the time, and that makes it exciting."

What high-net-worth personality is Frederick Ford?

- ❑ Family Steward
- ❑ Financial Phobic
- ❑ Independent
- ❑ the anonymous
- ❑ Mogul
- ❑ VIP
- ❑ Accumulator
- ❑ GAMBLER
- ❑ INNOVATOR

Client 3

Louis Brown is an executive in a high-technology firm. He was referred to you by one of your clients. When you contacted him, he said he would be willing to meet. On the phone he asks you to be ready to explain your thoughts on the Brinson Study.

You pass the security checkpoint. You walk into a nondescript conference room.

You start by explaining that the more you know about him and his investment goals, the more you both decide if it is a good fit. You ask the opening question, "What would you like your investing to achieve?" Lou says, "Perform." You think you know what he is, so you jump to Question 3. "How involved do you like to be in the investing process?" "Very involved," he responds. "I'm pretty technically oriented, and financial engineering interests me."

What high-net-worth personality is Louis Brown?

- ❑ FamilySteward
- ❑ **Financial PHOBIC**
- ❑ **Independent**
- ❑ **the** anonymous
- ❑ ***Mogul***
- ❑ VIP
- ❑ ACCUMULATOR
- ❑ GAMBLER
- ❑ INNOVATOR

Client 4

You have been referred to Gene Thompson by a client. You know he owns a local manufacturing plant and is active in Kiwanis. After making a number of calls, you were able to set up a meeting at his office. When you enter, you notice he is about 60 years old. As he walks over to greet you, you see that his shirt sleeves are rolled up and his jacket is off. His shoes are scuffed. There are pictures of very young children all around the office.

You ask about how he got started in the business, and then ask the first of the opening questions, "What would you like your investing to achieve?"

He responds, "Well, the business has taken pretty good care of me and Mary. Then it took pretty good care of our kids. And now that our kids have kids, I guess I'm looking to it to take care of them, too." And he points to the pictures.

What high-net-worth personality is Gene Thompson?

- ❑ FamilySteward
- ❑ Financial PHOBIC
- ❑ **Independent**
- ❑ theanonymous
- ❑ ***Mogul***
- ❑ VIP
- ❑ Accumulator
- ❑ GAMBLER
- ❑ INNOVATOR

Client 5

A friend of your mother's, Mary Ann Black, was recently widowed. Mr. Black had been a very successful entrepreneur. When he died, he left Mary the business interests as well as a substantial investment portfolio. Mary has told your mother she is at her wit's end dealing with all this. Your mother volunteers you to talk to her and help her sort out her financial situation. You go to Mary's house and sit on her yellow silk sofa. Chinese porcelains and oil paintings surround you. On the grand piano are silver-framed pictures of children.

After some light conversation you ask the first opening question, "What would you like your investing to achieve?" Mary laughs nervously and says, "Make money, I suppose."You use the follow-up question, "Do you want to make more money to take care of your family or be more independent yourself?" Mary looks around in some confusion. "Well both, I suppose. Would you like some iced tea?"

"No, thanks," you answer, then ask the next opening question, "When you think about money, what concerns, needs or feelings come to mind?" Mary is quick to respond, "Well, I don't like it at all. It is a lot to worry about, and Jim did it all, and I never knew what he was doing and I am so afraid of making a mistake." You go to the third opening question, "How involved do you want to be in the investing process?" Mary says, "If I could find someone I could trust, not at all."

What high-net-worth personality is Mary Ann Black?

- [ ] FamilySteward
- [ ] **Financial PHOBIC**
- [ ] **Independent**
- [ ] theanonymous
- [ ] ***Mogul***
- [ ] VIP
- [ ] ACCUMULATOR
- [ ] GAMBLER
- [ ] INNOVATOR

Client 6

Gary Antonelli is well known in the community because he is so active in local politics and economic development. You know him through a non-profit organization for which you volunteer.

You approach Gary about investing, and he is willing to meet with you. When you show up, the administrative assistant gets you settled in the chair in front of Gary's desk. He's running late which gives you a chance to examine the photographs of him taken with local politicians and community leaders. There are a dozen awards on the walls and in his credenza. When Gary comes in, he takes the chair behind his desk and says he has to take a quick call. In fact, he takes three in a row.

He turns to you and says, "Well. What do you have?" "As you know, I'm an investment advisor, but whether or not I have anything for you is what we have to sort out. Let me ask about your goal for your investment portfolio. What would you say is your primary goal? What do you want your investments to achieve?" "Increase in value, of course," he responds abruptly. Then you ask, "And when you think about those investments, your money, what concerns or needs come to mind?" "Well, for me, having money has always been about getting what I want. It puts me in the driver's seat."

What high-net-worth personality is Gary Antonelli?

- ❑ FamilySteward
- ❑ **Financial PHOBIC**
- ❑ **Independent**
- ❑ **the** anonymous
- ❑ ***Mogul***
- ❑ VIP
- ❑ ACCUMULATOR
- ❑ GAMBLER
- ❑ INNOVATOR

Client 7

Sheila Orzack is a management consultant referred to you by a client. You call her for weeks before you get through. She agrees to give you a few minutes, but isn't sure she will be looking for a new investment advisor. She drops a few names of prestigious investment management firms with which she has done business. When you enter her office you notice the furnishings and window treatments have clearly been coordinated by an interior designer. On the wall framed pictures of her with celebrities are hanging next to several original oil paintings. She wears tasteful, expensive clothes and gold jewelry.

After you compliment her on her office view, you explain you'd like to start with a few questions. "For example, what would you like your investing to achieve?" Sheila is clear, and says, "I want it to get bigger." You follow up with, "Do you want to make more money to take care of your family or be more independent yourself?" Sheila responds "I have kids, but they are on their own now, and I'd like to retire when the time is right. Actually I would like having more to invest in art ."

What high-net-worth personality is Shelia Orzack?

❑ FamilySteward

❑ **Financial PHOBIC**

❑ **Independent**

❑ theanonymous

❑ ***Mogul***

❑ VIP

❑ ACCUMULATOR

❑ GAMBLER

❑ INNOVATOR

Client 8

Richard Harkins, M.D. has signed up for your seminar on retirement planning for physicians. He is quiet during the meeting, but agrees to a follow-up meeting. When you finally get through to him by phone, he sounds busy and distracted but flattered. He is willing to give you a half hour.

You enter his office. His desk is obscured by reports and paper. The bookshelves are cluttered with binders. There is a framed photo on the bookshelf of a sailboat.

"You a sailor?" you ask. Dr. Harkins responds enthusiastically, "Absolutely. Ocean racing. Just finished the Newport run." You talk some more, then say, "Well, let's follow-up from that seminar. Let me start with this, "What would you like your investing to achieve?" Dr. Harkins looks a little confused, so you use the follow-up question to elaborate, "Is your goal for your investing to make money to take care of your family or to be financially independent yourself?"

Dr. Harkins says emphatically, "You got that right—financial independence. I went into medicine because I thought it was a calling, but managed care has me down. Now all I want to do is get enough together to sail full-time."

What high-net-worth personality is Dr. Harkins?

- ❑ FamilySteward
- ❑ **Financial PHOBIC**
- ❑ **Independent**
- ❑ theanonymous
- ❑ ***Mogul***
- ❑ VIP
- ❑ ACCUMULATOR
- ❑ GAMBLER
- ❑ INNOVATOR

Client 9

You meet Harry Smith briefly at a charity benefit and decide to follow up. Two weeks of calling and you can't get through. You discover that Harry's son went to your business school and you had the same finance course. You call up Harry's son who is working at the company and suggest that Harry's father might want to hear what you have to say. Harry's son sets up the meeting at their building. Harry meets you in a conference room. The top of the table is bare.

You start with your usual small talk and find Harry Smith hard to talk to. You switch to the opening question, "What would you like your investments to achieve?" He mentions performance. You don't get anything from the follow-up question.

You say, "People think differently about their portfolios. When you think about your investments, what needs or concerns come up for you?" He reiterates his point about performance. You say, "Since performance is important to you, how involved do you like to be in the investment process?" He says it depends. You decide to try the last question, "How important to you is the confidentiality of your financial affairs?" "He sits up, looks at you and says, "Nothing is more important."

What high-net-worth personality is Harry Smith?

- ❑ FamilySteward
- ❑ Financial PHOBIC
- ❑ Independent
- ❑ theanonymous
- ❑ Mogul
- ❑ VIP
- ❑ ACCUMULATOR
- ❑ GAMBLER
- ❑ INNOVATOR

Answers to High-Net-Worth IQ Quiz

Client 1

The first thing Tom Anders tells you is he's unhappy with the poor returns produced by his current investment advisor. When you meet, it's in a nondescript office in a nondescript building. He's certainly not spending his money on appearances. When you ask questions, he comes right out and tells you his priority—growing the assets.

Tom Anders is an ACCUMULATOR

Client 2

Frederick Ford's first question to you is about hedge funds. His second is about a just-announced merger. He subscribes to Bloomberg. When you ask him what interests him about investing he talks about the subtleties of portfolio performance measurement and style drift. What does he like about investing? The "wild ride" and the "excitement."

Frederick Ford is a GAMBLER

Client 3

Louis Brown has a technical background. He asks you about the Brinson study. Remember, most investors are not aware of the Brinson study and if they are, they are not inclined to talk about it. Also, he says he likes financial engineering.

Louis Brown is an INNOVATOR

Client 4

Gene Thompson has pictures of very young children all around his office. He mentions his family in the first few things he says to you. He describes his goal as wanting to structure his assets and those of his kids to take care of his family, especially the grandkids.

Gene Thompson is a FamilySteward

Client 5

Mary Ann Black is overwhelmed by the prospect of taking over the investment management from her late husband. Whenever you try to ask specifics about her financial goals she seems confused and changes the subject. She says she would like to find someone else to manage her money.

Mary Ann Black is a **Financial PHOBIC**

Client 6

Gary Antonelli is well known in local politics, economic development and non-profit circles. His office walls are covered with photographs of him taken with local politicians and community leaders and awards. He makes you wait while he takes calls. He is abrupt and to the point. He mentions being "in the driver's seat."

Gary Antonelli is a ***Mogul***

Client 7

Shelia Orzack is hard to reach. She makes it known that she is working with several prestigious investment management firms. Her office has been professionally decorated. She wears expensive clothes and gold jewelry. One of her goals is to build up her art collection.

Shelia Orzack is a VIP

Client 8

Richard Harkins, M.D. has a desk cluttered with reports and paper. He's an enthusiastic sailor. He wants nothing more than to sail full-time.

Dr. Harkins is an **Independent**

Client 9

Harry Smith meets you in a conference room, devoid of pictures or paper. He is difficult to draw out. Until you mention confidentiality, you can't get him to respond positively to anything.

Harry Smith is an a n o n y m o u s

The purpose of this exercise was to give you some practice at seeing that it is not all that difficult to accurately identify the high-net-worth personalities of affluent investors. While these examples are straightforward, investment advisors using high-net-worth psychology say identifying the types of their prospects and clients is fairly straightforward too.

What high-net-worth psychology does is to help systematize your relationship with prospects and clients, and insure you are focused on their wants and needs.

The Marketing Process

What does it really take to succeed—to excel—as an invest-ment advisor?

What does it really take to succeed—to excel—as an investment advisor targeting the affluent investor?

> ***"Vision without action is a daydream. Action without vision is a nightmare."***
> ***- Japanese proverb***

We've asked these questions of a number of investment advisors and we have received a wide range of answers. When we read and re-read these answers, we see that the answers fall into two broad categories:

1. Being good at managing money
2. Being good at marketing

This probably isn't news to you, but stop and think a minute. At which of these do you excel? In which have you received more training? Which is emphasized in the material you read?

If you are like most other advisors, you'll be better at, better trained in and more up-to-date on managing money. Marketing skills have traditionally not been emphasized in our industry.

However, today there is a different environment. There is much more competition for clients. Products are becoming commoditized. Technology is rearranging traditional industry structures. In the current environment, marketing turns out to be much more important than investment advisory ability.

Excelling in the Investment Advisory Business with the Affluent

To understand why marketing is the key success factor for an investment advisor targeting affluent investors, you have to understand what the investment advisory business is all about. Many might tell you it's about managing money for the well-to-do. Though this is correct, it is not the business model you need for the current environment.

The best business model for today's high-net-worth investment advisory business is not the management of money. Sure, the business model is about management, but it is about the management of client expectations. When we manage client expectations, we are marketing.

Of course, money management is entwined with the management of client expectations. However, we know that high-impact relationship management results in personal introductions and client referrals as well as more assets from existing clients regardless of investment performance.

Admittedly, certain high-net-worth personalities are more sensitive to investment performance (e.g., Accumulators). Even in these cases, high-impact relationship management can mitigate the adverse impact of poor investment performance.

However, before we get to the point where we take action to be sure our clients are highly satisfied, we have to find them. Investment performance, even stunning investment performance, is not enough these days to attract new affluent clients.

A wealthy investor must be motivated to entrust his wealth to you. The investment advisor targeting private wealth will focus less on investment performance and more on marketing. Marketing is about finding, winning and keeping affluent investors. Marketing is the critical success factor; marketing is the difference among so-so, good and great. Marketing expertise enables investment advisors to excel and to reach the top rungs in the industry.

We also need to be clear about the role of investment performance. It's important, very important. Over the long-term, solid investment performance will dramatically affect the success of an investment advisor. Moreover, it's your ethical responsibility to strive to achieve the best investment performance for every one of your clients, taking their unique situations into account.

The Marketing Process

What is the marketing process? It's the cycle you go through to build your investment advisory business.

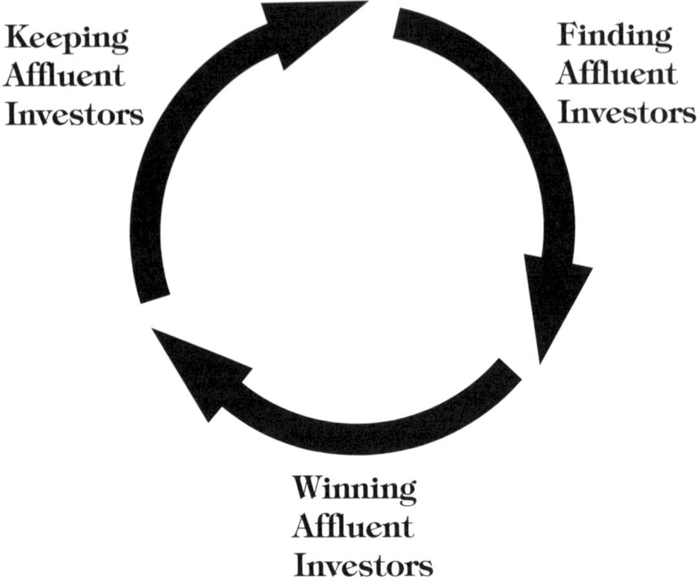

We begin the cycle with finding affluent investors, which is the prospecting phase. As we will see, there are many ways of prospecting for the rich. Some strategies work far better than others, especially personal introductions and client referrals.

High-net-worth psychology can help you find new clients, especially the type of affluent investor with whom you work best. High-net-worth psychology also is effective in helping you recognize which prospecting strategy to use depending on the type of client you are targeting. In Section II of this book, we examine all the commonly used prospecting strategies and focus on those that have been shown to be most effective in reaching new affluent investors.

Once you've located a wealthy prospect, you need to convert that prospect into a client. In other words, you need to win them over, and the best way to do so is by communicating to them in ways that matter most.

Again, high-net-worth psychology is important in the process. High-net-worth psychology enables you to confidently position yourself, your services and investment products to prospects and new clients. You do not have to change your approach to investing. What high-net-worth psychology does is help you potentially do a better job for wealthy clients because you have a deeper understanding of their goals and needs. High-net-worth psychology allows you to communicate with affluent investors on their level. In Section III of this book, we discuss how to most effectively position the typical products and services that investment advisors provide.

Finding and winning affluent clients is not enough. You have to keep them and if you want to keep them, you must continue to invest in your relationships with them. Throughout your time with your clients, your number one objective is to satisfy them. Investment performance—even great investment performance—is rarely enough to elicit complete satisfaction. In Section IV of this book, we focus on keeping clients through high-impact relationship management.

High-net-worth psychology is critical if you want to keep affluent

investors regardless of years of investment performance. With high-net-worth psychology, you will know how to relate to each wealthy investor based on their primary motivation for investing.

We picture the process as a circle because highly satisfied, wealthy clients can help you find new wealthy clients through personal introductions and referrals.

We've included the final section of this book (Section V) because client-focused marketing plans are the tactical way to implement this three-stage marketing process. Client-focused marketing plans are being adopted by elite financial advisors because it is proven they get results and get them quickly.

> ***"We despise no source that can pay us pleasing attention."***
> ***—Mark Twain***

The first section of this book explored the worlds of wealth and the psychology of the affluent. Because good marketing is 1% information and 99% implementation, we devote the rest of the book to implementation issues.

II

Finding Affluent Investors

Prospecting Strategies

We are constantly asked for the secret to prospecting, for the silver bullet, for the fail-safe solution. Everyone wants to know if there is some miraculous formula to make prospecting easy.

Let's face it. The hardest part of financial services business is prospecting. Our research shows that investment advisors, brokers, insurance agents and private bankers agree that prospecting for new wealthy clients is the single most difficult part of their business.

> ***"True wealth is not a static thing. It is a living thing made out of the disposition of people to create and to distribute the good things of life and rising standards of living."***
>
> ***- Franklin Delano Roosevelt***

Why is it so difficult? It's hard because most affluent investors are not in the market for a new investment advisor. Although you are looking for new wealthy clients, the fact is that these affluent investors are NOT necessarily looking for you.

If you're like most investment advisors, you still want to build up your investment advisory business. While you can meet some of your growth goals through asset capture, you also need to prospect for new clients.

Qualified Leads

When we talk about prospecting among affluent investors, we have to be precise. One investment advisor said to us, "If they can fog a mirror, they're potential clients." In reality, it's not worth your time to prospect for anyone who is not a qualified lead.

What is a qualified lead? A qualified lead needs what you have to offer, has the assets to make it worthwhile for you and is motivated to act now. A qualified lead is:

1. A wealthy investor who requires investment advisory services. For many reasons, not all wealthy investors have an interest in high-quality professional investment advisory services. Clearly, you want to direct your marketing efforts to reach those who do.

2. A wealthy investor that has the requisite financial resources. Many investment advisors work with minimum account sizes. To be a qualified lead, the affluent investor must meet your minimums.

3. A wealthy investor that is interested in talking to you now. It's not enough that the high-net-worth individual requires investment advisory services, or that he or she meets your minimum account size. The wealthy investor must be interested in talking to you and doing something today.

Now that we have defined qualified leads, let's get them into your high-net-worth prospect pool. In the best situation you:

- Get your wealthy clients to personally introduce you to other wealthy investors.

- Get your wealthy clients to refer you to other wealthy investors.

These two interrelated prospecting strategies are extremely effective. When you get the top advisors in this business to tell you how they became successful, they will say, "My clients built my business," or "Clients introduce me to other clients," or "It may seem slow, but in the long run, client referrals and personal introductions are the best way to go." Think about growing clients the way you project asset growth. Both growth curves start off slow, but rise exponentially over time.

While personal introductions and client referrals are the optimal prospecting strategies, we should not disregard some other approaches. Though just about anything can work, that's not the point. The issue is which approaches are cost-effective for the way you do business.

Let's take a systematic look at some of the more common prospecting strategies and their cost-effectiveness. Though your primary prospecting goal is to find approaches that are cost-effective, the secondary benefit value of any prospecting strategy is its long-term worth in positioning you as a high-quality investment advisor.

Evaluating Prospecting Strategies

Our sole focus is those affluent investors who will entrust their portfolios to you. We are not interested in the "self-directed"

millionaire investors, because you cannot earn satisfactory fee or commission income from "self-directed" investors. What we will do is evaluate the seven prospecting strategies in use today in terms of their effectiveness in placing you in front of affluent investor prospects. The seven prospecting strategies are:

- Personal introductions and client referrals;
- Advisor referrals;
- Seminars;
- Public relations;
- Advertising;
- Direct mail; and
- Cold calling.

Personal Introductions and Client Referrals

These are usually the most cost-effective ways to obtain new affluent investor clients. This bears repeating. Save for rare circumstances, personal introductions are the undisputed, number one way to grow an investment advisory practice. Client referrals are cousins of personal introductions.

A personal introduction occurs when one of your affluent clients directly introduces you to other wealthy investors. For instance, if you, your wealthy client and one of his or her affluent peers go to lunch together with the explicit intent of that lunch being an

introduction of you and that friend, we have a personal introduction.

A client referral is somewhat less powerful. In a referral situation, your client may provide a name for you to call, or go one step further and set the stage for you to call. However, your client does not personally participate in the initial meeting.

> Just how effective is a referral? Let's benchmark your own practice. Let's say you have 100 very satisfied clients. From those 100 clients, how many new clients would you expect to get next year from introductions and referrals?

Here is convincing data on the effectiveness of introductions and referrals.

Top investment advisors are able to obtain 66 new wealthy investor clients for every 100 satisfied wealthy investor clients. This means it is possible to grow your affluent client base by 66% a year, and your assets by at least that much. Keep in mind, however, that this figure represents the very best in this industry, and you may not be there just yet. These numbers do reveal something about the cost-effectiveness of introductions and referrals as a prospecting system. They work.

To elicit personal introductions and make client referrals work, you have to do two things. One, the wealthy clients you approach must be very satisfied with their relationship with you. Being very satisfied goes beyond investment performance. Being very satisfied means that they value the quality of their interpersonal relationship with you.

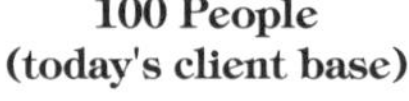

100 People
(today's client base)

166 People
(next year's client base)

Here is the magic. Most clients only think about their personal relationship with you when it comes to being willing to make an introduction or referral.

We have proof. As you would expect, few well-to-do clients who are unhappy and dissatisfied with their relationship with their investment advisors are willing to make referrals; every 100 dissatisfied clients result in just 15 referrals for their advisors in a year's time. Why would anybody dissatisfied with their relationship with their advisor recommend him or her to their peers, friends and family? When investment performance is truly exceptional, that's when.

You can just about double this baseline referral rate if your clients are all fairly satisfied. Every 100 generally satisfied clients result in 26 new client referrals for their investment advisors.

However, as the following Exhibit shows, the real payoff is in rendering your current clients VERY satisfied. Every 100 very satisfied clients result in 66 new client referrals for their advisors. What is the implication of this number for your practice? A potential 66% growth rate in your client base in a single year. For most investment advisors, that kind of growth means never doing any other form of prospecting.

Number of Client Referrals per 100 Current Clients in One Year

Of course, and here is the second thing you must do, you must ask for the referral. Wealthy clients rarely wake up one morning and think, "I haven't given Sam a referral lately, maybe I should work on it." While some affluent clients will refer other wealthy investors to you without your asking, this is the exception, not the rule. If you want personal introductions and referrals, you need to be proactive. You have to ask. In researching the best practices of financial advisors who consistently get referrals, we find they all employ a similar approach. They set the stage for referrals, directly ask and then provide feedback (as we will discuss in the next chapter).

The process of asking for personal introductions and client referrals also creates significant secondary value for you. It is a very powerful form of word-of-mouth marketing. You're creating a buzz in the "right circles". If wealthy investors are talking about you and saying good things, then you're going to get even more business over the long run.

Advisor Referrals

Advisor referrals are generally the next most effective way of procuring new wealthy investor clients. In the case of the Anonymous, it is essentially the only way to reach them. Professional advisors have strong relationships with their affluent clients, and if they refer their clients to you, you have a very good shot at the business.

There are a number of different advisors who can provide you with high-quality qualified leads. Accountants, attorneys, fundraisers in charitable organizations, life insurance agents, property/casualty insurance agents and even travel agents can offer promising leads to new affluent clients. Of all of these, accountants are probably the best advisor from whom to receive referrals because accountants generally have the strongest relationships with their affluent clients.

More and more investment advisors these days are approaching accountants to win referrals. In addition, some accountants are becoming competitors by entering the investment advisory business themselves.

Regardless of the professional advisor you have targeted, you can use a number of ways to motivate them to refer wealthy investors to you. Some of the most effective approaches are joint-marketing programs and technical education programs. Though these take a lot of time to develop and deliver, advisors are looking for people who will help them solve one of the problems in their practices—prospecting for new clients. Cross-referrals sound appealing, but rarely work out to be equal and this imbalance can cause bad feelings. We discuss advisor referrals in greater detail in a later chapter.

Aside from being able to garner new business, by working through advisors you are positioning yourself as an expert within the

community of professionals who serve the affluent—the secondary benefit of this prospecting strategy. Your professional stature can be greatly enhanced by the working relationships you develop with other top professionals.

Seminars

Seminars can be extremely useful in screening and especially in motivating certain prospective wealthy investors. As with any business development activity, success is a function of execution. Unfortunately, when it comes to conducting seminars for the affluent, research indicates that most investment advisors are doing a poor job. However, this opens an opportunity for you.

There is one and only one purpose of having a seminar—to end up in a one-to-one meeting with an affluent prospect. Too many investment advisors forget this and try to sell investment products in a seminar. We have seen hundreds of product-oriented seminars (e.g. large-cap mutual funds or variable annuities or Alaskan trusts) for every seminar that is truly process-oriented (e.g. about estate management or tax-sensitive investing or asset protection planning).

The content of the seminar has to be in synch with the interests of your affluent audience. Seminars provide another good example of where high-net-worth psychology comes into play. In one instance, we created an entire marketing program around private foundations for one of our investment advisor clients. Clearly, he is not promoting private foundations to Accumulators. When positioning the idea to the other personalities he does so very differently depending on with whom he is speaking. For instance, for Family Stewards, he will explain that a private foundation is a way to pass on the values of giving to the next generation as well as to have the family involved in a very positive activity. For VIPs, he will explain ways in which a foundation can carry on their name and positive impact far into the future. When he is meeting with a Mogul, he will show that a private foundation is a means of achieving a measure of control.

In a seminar, the most effective approach is to introduce people to benefits and solutions. You want to introduce them to new ways of thinking about their investment portfolios in ways consistent with their high-net-worth personalities. Once they become interested, it is easier to secure a one-to-one meeting. It is in that one-to-one meeting where you determine if you and the affluent investor should work together, not in the seminar.

To make more affluent prospects comfortable with you, seminars should be small, even somewhat intimate, and interactive whenever possible. This way, prospective wealthy investor clients are able to learn more effectively, grow accustomed to working with you, get a feel for your personal style and be in a better position to decide if they want to know more.

Looking further down the road, seminars are a great way to sensitize prospective wealthy investor clients to your services. Well-executed seminars for the affluent can help create a buzz as well as make you a top choice when an audience member, even years later, decides to take action.

Public Relations

We recommend that all investment advisors conduct some type of public relations program. For many investment advisors, occasional bylined articles, newsletters and even a book are possibilities. Writing is a great way to position your expertise. Easier still are speaking engagements which are very effective and shorter-term ways of helping you position yourself. The investment advisory industry is becoming all the more competitive. Skillful public relations is an excellent way of positioning yourself as an expert.

A great advantage of public relations is that it is underutilized in the industry.

Do not expect that putting your efforts into public relations will attract walk-in wealthy investor clients. In general, it will not, although there is always the exception. However, putting your efforts into public relations can dramatically increase your closing rate and considerably strengthen your relationship with other professional advisors.

Advertising

Advertising also will unlikely bring you new affluent investor clients. A few leading financial institutions with international reputations and prestige (such as J.P. Morgan, U.S. Trust and Bessemer Trust) have had some success with advertising. However, for individual investment advisors, advertising has little primary value in terms of bringing in wealthy investors.

Advertising can be beneficial as a supplement to your other endeavors. It can be useful in supporting your efforts to be seen as an expert. Like public relations, it can significantly help your closing rate. It can also be effective in reinforcing to wealthy investor clients that they made a good decision in coming to you.

Direct Mail

Our studies of direct mail show it is even less effective than public relations and advertising in generating new business from affluent investors. The reason is that the wealthy receive many direct mail appeals daily, and are used to ignoring them.

Worse yet, direct mail is hard to do well. The message must be persuasive enough to generate action, and most direct mail pieces do not. We have seen a few drip-marketing programs that have brought in new affluent clients, but they were expensive and they carried a long time frame.

Cold Calling

When it comes to wealthy investors, cold calling rarely, if ever, works. This is especially true if an advisor is promoting fee-based investment advisory services as opposed to the latest hot stock.

To date, the one exception is change-of-circumstance situations. For instance, when business owners sell their businesses and become liquid millionaires, they might be open to a cold call from a "name" institution.

We know an entrepreneur named Mike who sold his software firm. After the sale was reported in *The Wall Street Journal,* he was called by at least 14 financial professionals from firms like Credit Suisse, Morgan Stanley, Goldman Sachs and Bankers Trust. Morgan won the business. This form of cold calling can result in some new wealthy clients, but it is proving less effective as more and more investment advisors focus on change-of-circumstance situations.

"They all started out with nothing in those days and the biggest crooks won. I was just lucky to come from a line of successful crooks."
- Marshall Field, V

The following table summarizes the primary and secondary value of the seven prospecting strategies we discussed.

The Value of Various Prospecting Strategies

Prospecting Strategy	Primary Value	Secondary Value
Personal introductions and client referrals	Best means of prospecting for wealthy investors.	Enhances image through word-of-mouth marketing.
Advisor referrals	Can result in a steady stream of new wealthy investor clients.	Creates a position of expertise in the community.
Seminars	Excellent screening and motivating strategy for wealthy prospects.	Sensitizes prospective wealthy clients to your services.
Public relations	Unlikely to result in new wealthy investors.	Excellent strategy to enhance your positioning as an investment advisor.
Advertising	Yet even more unlikely to result in new wealthy clients.	Can enhance your image as an investment advisor.
Direct mail	More unlikely to result in new wealthy clients.	More limited impact.
Cold calling	You probably have a better chance winning the lottery.	Miniscule.

Always use the discipline of thinking of all prospecting strategies in a cost-effectiveness framework. Ask yourself, what will each strategy yield in terms of incremental new clients? Be sure to factor in the cost of your time in addition to direct expenses.

While there are many ways to generate new business, the repeatedly demonstrated single most effective (and cost-effective) way is through personal introductions and referrals from your current affluent clients. We strongly recommend that you focus on personal introductions and referrals in your market development plan and that you place them at the core of your prospecting efforts.

At the same time, there are other prospecting strategies that you can use to build your investment advisory business. Referrals from other advisors is very effective as are well-designed seminars.

A third leg of your strategy should be building your image. This is the role of public relations and to a lesser degree, advertising, both of which will facilitate growing your investment advisory business.

Personal Introductions and Referrals

While there are many ways to generate new investment advisory business, one of the best ways is by gaining new clients. As we saw in the last chapter, probably the most cost-effective way to capture new wealthy clients is through personal introductions and referrals. We believe that all investment advisors should incorporate client introductions and referrals in their market development plans and in their prospecting strategies.

> ***"Money is better than poverty, if only for financial reasons."***
>
> ***- Woody Allen***

We showed you in Chapter 6 the importance of high levels of client satisfaction. We are also emphasizing it in this chapter. Why? Unless your wealthy client is highly satisfied with their interpersonal relationship with you, it is extremely unlikely that you'll get any personal introductions or referrals. While sensational investment performance may, once in a while, result in personal introductions and client referrals, you should not bet your business on it. Investment

advisors who have excellent rapport are far more likely to obtain introductions and referrals from current clients.

You also have to ask for what you want, and what you want is the personal introduction and referral. The six-step process described in the following pages is what many of the top advisors do to secure a constant and profitable stream of introductions and referrals from their wealthy clients. However, before discussing the six-step process, let's look at who can and is likely to provide you with personal introductions and referrals.

Using High-Net-Worth Psychology to Get Personal Introductions and Client Referrals

Think of one of your top 10 wealthy clients. What high-net-worth personalities do they have?

Now think about their social networks. To which organizations do they belong? Where do they work? To which non-profits do they give or for which ones do they volunteer? Who do they know? What are their interests?

Yet, in thinking of these people, how willing would they be to refer you to or introduce you to someone they know?

Different high-net-worth personalities have different attitudes towards making introductions and referrals. Some types of affluent investors have large networks they could plug you into, and other types have smaller social networks, or none at all like the Anonymous.

Also, different personalities have different preconceived notions towards making personal introductions and referrals.

The following table summarizes the differences in high-net-worth personalities with respect to personal introductions and client referrals.

Using High-Net-Worth Psychology to Get Personal Introductions and Client Referrals

High-Net-Worth Personality	Social Ties	Willingness to Introduce/Refer
Family Stewards	Strong	High
VIPs	Strong	Medium
Moguls	Strong	Medium
Independents	Medium	High
Gamblers	Medium	High
Innovators	Medium	High
Accumulators	Medium	Medium
Financial Phobics	Medium	Low
The Anonymous	Low	Low

FamilySteward

Family Stewards are great for personal introductions and client referral development. They tend to be well connected in their communities and have extensive social networks.

Because so many Family Stewards own small, community-based businesses, they have developed these social networks to support their business interests. It is common for Family Stewards to belong to community organizations, such as the Rotary Club and the Chamber of Commerce, and they are often found on boards of local non-profits.

Family Stewards know many people who would make great investment advisory clients.

The good news is that Family Stewards are also quite willing to provide personal introductions and referrals of their friends and business associates. Family Stewards are generally loyal and helpful by nature. If they like how you work with them, they trust you will do well with their friends and peers. Family Stewards will acknowledge how you have helped them and will feel that a personal introduction or a referral serves as a thank you for the extra services you have performed for them.

VIPs

VIPs are also well connected. However, unlike Family Stewards, who are well connected because it helps business, VIPs are well connected because of the status they seek among their peers. They like knowing important people and like being thought of as important.

They have extensive social networks and know a lot of people to whom you would like to be introduced. VIPs are somewhat more lukewarm to the idea of personal introductions and referrals, though. They would be more willing to make personal introductions and referrals if they can see how their own prestige would be enhanced.

Moguls

Moguls have extensive social networks. Given their drive for control, they invest time in strong personal and professional networks as an extension of their influence and power. These networks are likely to be highly personal. Moguls generally are not group oriented and rarely serve in community organizations.

As a result, Moguls are less likely to leverage these networks on your behalf, unless there is some way they also can benefit. If they sense they will gain an advantage if they introduce or refer you to someone, they will do so. Thus, you need to create a clearly defined win-win scenario in order to motivate Moguls to procure for you new affluent investor clients.

Independents

Independents have average social networks. Their closest connections will center around their hobbies or avocations such as sailing, golfing or art collecting. They will know other people as committed to personal goals as they are. If they are satisfied with your services, they happily will make an introduction or referral.

GAMBLERS

Like many others of the nine high-net-worth personalities, Gamblers have social networks about average in size. Many people in these

networks share the Gambler's obsession with the stock market and investing. Because of their high involvement with investing, Gamblers are highly motivated to refer you to others who share these same interests.

INNOVATORS

Innovators are generally pretty solitary people. As a result, their social networks are somewhat more modest. On the other hand, they are extremely enthusiastic and involved in investing. If they have come to trust and rely on you, they will be highly motivated to refer you to other people they know.

Many Innovators have technical backgrounds and might be computer specialists or engineers. They will know similar career people, through inventor or entrepreneurial networks, or through their high-technology industry contacts.

ACCUMULATORS

Accumulators have social networks about average in size. Accumulators are a diverse group, so it is harder to typify the people in their networks except that they generally have more modest life styles. Accumulators tend not to spend on things.

Accumulators are willing to refer you to others if they are satisfied with your work for them. Remember that their main criterion is investment performance. You'll be well advised to make your requests

for introductions and referrals at times when you deliver excellent portfolio performance results.

Financial PHOBICS

In general, Financial Phobics have comparatively small social networks. These tend to consist of close friends and family and a few business associates. It's also likely that many of the members of a Financial Phobics social network are as wealthy as they are.

However, the likelihood is low that they will refer you to people in their social or professional network. Financial Phobics dislike talking about investments and are unlikely to know enough about the investment situation of their friends to be able to make an introduction or referral.

the anonymous

The Anonymous are extremely close-mouthed about investing—investments per se as well as the investment advisors with whom they work. They also often have limited social networks, because of their avoidance of close contact with others.

Even if these networks were extensive, it wouldn't make sense for you to ask an Anonymous for a referral. They won't make one because it would violate their privacy. The best policy is not to ask because asking for personal introductions and client referrals will only hurt your relationship with the Anonymous. The best way to seek referrals and introductions with this group is by establishing an effective professional advisor referral network.

How You Can Make Personal Introductions and Referrals Happen

Of course, once in a while a highly satisfied client will make an unsolicited referral. However, why would you depend on such a dicey prospecting strategy when you can create a big pipeline of wealthy new investors by being proactive?

If your highly satisfied wealthy clients are asked (and asked in the proper way), they will come through with referrals and personal introductions. We found this when we studied how the best investment advisors managed to hit exceptionally high referral rates year after year.

It turns out they use a similar process to get personal introductions and referrals. We have boiled down that process into six steps. There are no great secrets to asking for and getting personal introductions and client referrals. As always, the key is consistency.

As we noted, these six steps emerged from intensive studies of the top investment advisors, the ones we call the "best of the best." You can build a tremendous investment advisory business following these six steps, especially if you add your own style. Think of these six steps as an outline that you will adapt based on the way you like to work.

The six steps to the art of getting referrals and introductions are:

- Step #1: Set expectations.
- Step #2: Keep tabs on client satisfaction.
- Step #3: Ask for the personal introduction or referral.
- Step #4: Thank them for the personal introduction or referral.
- Step #5: Tell them what happened.
- Step #6: Thank them again.

Your personality and style will make the framework unique to you. As you become more skilled at obtaining affluent investor personal introductions and referrals, continue to modify the six-step framework to create a personal approach that works best for you.

Step #1: Set Expectations

Optimally, you want to create the right set of client expectations from the beginning of every relationship. From the start, explain to your affluent clients that you will be checking in frequently to gauge their satisfaction. Tell them how important this is to you and that they can expect you to ask how things are going from time to time. Unless you receive continual and honest feedback from your clients, you won't know how satisfied they are, and you won't know how to increase their satisfaction.

The best advisors also take the time at the beginning of the relationship to let their clients know that they appreciate personal introductions and referrals. These advisors find that some wealthy clients generate several personal introductions and referrals a year. Gaining a new client via referrals creates the perfect opportunity to create expectations for later referrals.

Step #2: Keep Tabs on Client Satisfaction

Now that you have set the stage for receiving feedback on client satisfaction, when do you want feedback?

As you work with affluent investors there will be obvious times in the relationship when asking for feedback is natural. Ask for feedback after you have performed a major service for the client. Other good times come after significant increases in the value of their portfolios, completion of a planning process, investing new assets and rebalancing their portfolios. After each significant interaction, it is important that you solicit feedback.

Obviously, the best feedback is a compliment. Who doesn't love a compliment? But don't stop there. Talk with your wealthy client until you find at least one thing you can improve upon in a tangible way. Remember, you welcome negative or constructive feedback, or how else can you improve? Affluent investors understand that things can and do go wrong, and look for your efforts for confirmation. Often the most satisfied clients are the ones who have been through difficult periods with you.

Once you have found at least one thing you can improve for the client, be certain to fix it. Nothing will gratify them more.

Elite financial advisors often set aside the time for an in-person review with each of their significant high-net-worth clients. In this meeting, they concentrate on reviewing their relationship with these clients. Depending on circumstances, these elite financial advisors go over the investment performance and other events in the account. Then they review the relationship by soliciting feedback again.

This step enables you to get an exact fix on client satisfaction and to gauge the strength of the relationship. Once you know your client is very satisfied, move to Step #3. If your client is not very satisfied, you must render them satisfied before you can move any further in this process.

Step #3: Ask for the Personal Introduction or Referral

Frankly, it is rare for clients to wake up one morning and think about providing personal introductions or referrals to their investment advisors. You have to take the initiative if you want the introduction or referral.

But how do you ask? Simply asking affluent clients if they know of someone who can use your services is not very effective. All too often you get "no" for an answer. This approach generally fails because you are forcing your affluent clients to deal with two issues simultaneously. You are asking them who might need your investment services and whether or not they would feel comfortable with making an introduction or referral of that person. You can increase your effectiveness by separating these two questions.

Enter high-net-worth psychology. By using high-net-worth psychology you can be much more effective in how you ask for personal introduction and referrals.

Here is the game plan. Talk about the benefits of your investment services from the perspective of the affluent individual's high-net-worth personality. Wealthy investors tend to know other affluent investors with the same high-net-worth personality. Focus on high-net-worth psychology and their reasons for investing. You can better customize your approach to asking for the referral this way. For example, in talking to a Family Steward you might explain "I'm a family man and so are you. I really enjoy dealing with clients like you and helping take care of your family. If you know anyone else in need of this type of expertise..."

Step #4: Thank Them for the Personal Introduction or Referral

The thing to recognize is that there is social cost to your affluent clients for providing you with a personal introduction or referral. You should quickly reciprocate and show gratitude. A quick, handwritten note, for example, is appropriate. George Bush was famous for his handwritten notes, and this personal touch made him popular among politicians and world leaders.

Thanking your clients for personal introductions and referrals provides you with another opportunity to maintain contact. At the same time, you also are intensifying your relationship with them.

Step #5: Tell Them What Happened

Your affluent client (the one that made the personal introduction or referral) will be curious how things went. It's important that you let them know that things went well, but be mindful about confidentiality.

In the case of referrals, for instance, one of the first things your affluent client will want to know is whether or not you were able to make contact with the person. They also will want to be reassured that the initial meeting went well. One way to provide feedback is to send your client another quick note. Notes are better than telephone calls because they do not have to be returned and you can avoid playing telephone tag. Of course, you will want to make some of these follow-up contacts over the phone to explore whether any new needs have arisen as well as to build on your existing relationship.

It is important to protect the confidentiality of the prospect. Never disclose personal information or the business of one client to another.

If you do, the client you tell will rightly assume you are as careless with their own personal information, leading to immediate dissatisfaction.

Step #6: Thank Them Again

Just because you thanked your client for the referral once, don't stop there. Thank them again. Especially thank them if you close some business.

Unless clients are truly happy with their personal relationship with you, you will not receive many referrals. Therefore, the essential first step is to make sure all your top clients are as satisfied as possible with their relationship with you. Investment advisors who have excellent rapport are much more likely to obtain many personal introductions and referrals from current clients.

You also have to ask for what you want, and what you want is the personal introduction or referral. The six-step process is how elite financial advisors obtain a constant (and profitable) stream of new wealthy investor clients from their existing clientele.

> ***"When money talks, no one notices what grammar it uses."***
> ***- Anonymous***

Keep in mind that high-net-worth psychology will help you in this process as it will help you anticipate who else

your clients know (who is in their social networks) and how to ask for referrals (and who not to approach).

Referrals From Other Advisors

Next to personal introductions and referrals from clients, introductions and referrals through advisors are usually the next most cost-effective method of prospecting. The wealthy trust their advisors, and will trust them to make good referrals. If those referrals can be directed your way, it's a great means to build your business.

The trick is how you can get these introductions and referrals.

Stop for a minute and think about how people find investment advisors. How have your clients found you?

> ***"Money, it turns out, was like sex. You thought of nothing else if you didn't have it and thought of other things if you did."***
> ***- James Baldwin***

People are careful with their money, so they often check around. They ask friends, co-workers and family and they ask their other advisors, attorneys, accountants or insurance agents. Professional advisors all have networks of other advisors they introduce and refer people to, and from whom they receive introductions and referrals. Your challenge is to become a part of the professional referral network of several advisors.

There are several types of professional advisors you should consider. Among the professional advisors who make referrals to investment advisors are:

- Accountants;
- Attorneys;
- Life Insurance agents;
- Managers in non-profits; and
- Property/casualty agents.

Of these, you should consider focusing on accountants and attorneys. Let's look at each in turn.

Accountants

Almost all accountants regularly refer their clients to investment advisors. In fact, our research has found that 93% of all accountants refer at least one client to an investment advisor every year. Many refer more than one.

This high percentage is the best reason for you to develop these relationships with accountants. When accountants recommend investment advisors, they usually recommend only one (68%). This is enormously advantageous because clients are likely to follow-through on a recommendation of a trusted advisor. The research

backs up this claim. In fact, three out of four people select the investment advisor the accountant recommended.

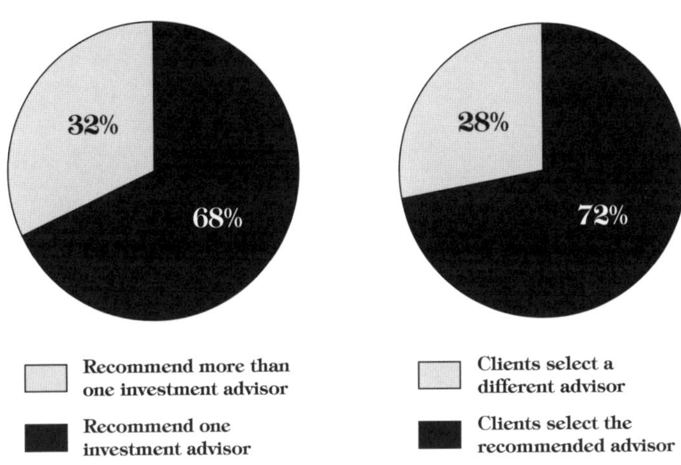

There is one complication you should consider in thinking about strategic alliances with accountants. Accountants could be your competitors as they have come to realize the attractiveness of the investment advisory business themselves.

Accountants know they have influence over their clients and know the investment advisory business is often more profitable than the accounting business. Currently, two-thirds of accountants (61%) are trying to figure out how they can more directly participate in the investment advisory business, although most (92%) are not looking to get into portfolio management.

Attorneys

Attorneys also make referrals, but need to be approached and worked with differently. Like accountants, most attorneys (86%) make referrals. However, unlike accountants, almost all attorneys will suggest several investment advisors (83%) for their clients to consider. Attorneys make multiple referrals because they need to keep their distance from the selection process (if things don't work out with the new investment advisor, attorneys do not want their clients angry with them).

How Attorneys Recommend Investment Advisors

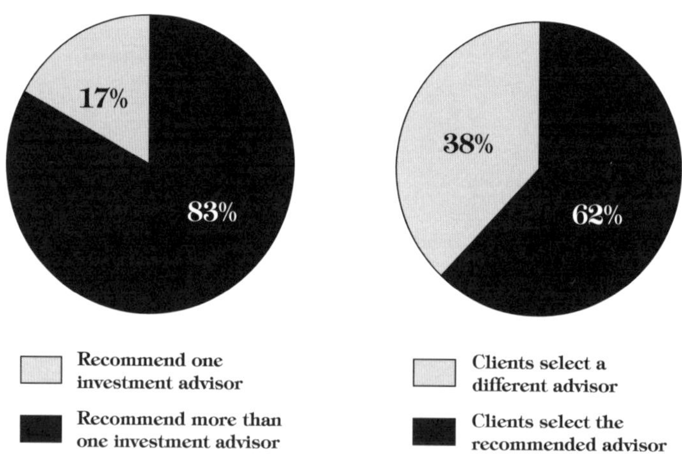

Although clients referred by attorneys will evaluate several different investment advisors in their selection process, most ultimately will select one of the investment advisors suggested by the attorney (62%). It may be advisable to convince an attorney of your expertise and professionalism with the end goal having them give you first billing among a set of referrals.

Professionals other than accountants and attorneys should come second regarding important relationships you should develop for referrals. Insurance agents (life and property/casualty agents) have many clients, but their relationships with those clients are often more episodic than the prolonged relationships of accountants and attorneys. As a result, they often don't know whether their clients are in need of an investment advisor, and their clients don't always think of approaching them when they have that sort of question. There is an even more problematic issue. Increasingly, many life insurance producers are becoming investment advisors themselves, and therefore won't refer to you or any other investment advisor.

Also consider managers in non-profits among these professionals in your second tier. They often do not have the close advisory relationships (and therefore the trust) with affluent people as do accountants and attorneys. However, if you develop a charitable estate planning component to your practice, these people will become important in your market development strategy.

Developing Referral Relationships with Advisors

Now that you have an understanding of with whom you should develop relationships, let's get down to the how. It is a three-step process:

- Step #1: Identify accountant and attorney candidates.

- Step #2: Develop a relationship enhancement plan for each accountant and attorney on your list.
- Step #3: Implement your relationship enhancement plans.

Step #1: Identify Accountant and Attorney Candidates

The first step is to identify accountant and attorney relationships you could develop into the kind of strategic alliances that result in referrals. Start by writing down a few (say, three) accounting and legal firms or people you think have potential.

It would be wise, for example, to focus on firms which have a large number of small business-owning clients (as opposed to corporate clients or criminal work) because people who own small businesses are more likely to be wealthy and good prospects for you. It's also good to project the number of referrals they might be able to provide. Base your projection on what you know about their clientele and the current strength of your relationships with the professionals in those firms.

Step #2: Develop a Relationship Enhancement Plan for Each Accountant and Attorney on Your List

The second step is to develop relationship enhancement plans. Create a relationship enhancement plan for each firm on your list.

This plan should start with who you know and who you want to know better. It should also profile the services the firm offers and the markets to which they offer those services. For example, you may discover that one legal firm specializes in trusts and estates and another in pension and benefit planning. The most important component of your plan should be to figure out why the professionals in that firm should work with you (more about this later in the chapter).

Step #3: Implement Your Relationship Enhancement Plans

The third step is to put your plan in place. It will take time to develop these relationships—trust is not created quickly and professionals will have to trust you immensely before they send their clients to you.

Once your personal relationships with some of the individuals in the firm are developed, you could first feel them out and approach them with a customized package. This package should have several components, including your background and professional qualifications, the services you offer and how you and the firm can work together.

Bring Value

There are four ways investment advisors have developed to work with accounting and legal firms to obtain personal introductions and referrals. These methods include:

- Joint-marketing programs;
- Providing technical or marketing education;
- Cross-referral arrangements; and

- Fee-sharing or other compensation.

All of these are effective, depending on the firms and professionals involved. However, we have found the most effective of these are joint-marketing programs, and we will look at those first.

Joint-Marketing Programs

Joint-marketing programs are efforts that you and the firm undertake together to generate new prospects and clients for you both. These often are seminar programs offered to a targeted list, but they also can be one-on-one joint marketing.

We know one investment advisor who has teamed up with a legal firm to offer seminars in how to create private foundations. This is a highly specialized area that attracts high-net-worth clients and which can result in substantial legal business as well as assets to manage.

We have also seen accountants, law firms and investment advisors team up to offer programs targeted at the unique issues of family businesses. Another area garnering increasing attention is deferred compensation. Here, the accountants design the plan and are responsible for administration. The attorneys also can play a role in the design work but are responsible for the legal documents. The investment advisor manages the money in Rabbi trusts. This is just one example of three professionals—you, an attorney and an accountant—joining to service one project.

Accountants and attorneys like joint-marketing programs, particularly if they can sense that you will also put forth a lot of effort. Both of these professions are highly competitive, and both are finding it difficult to attract new clients—especially wealthy clients. They have the same challenges you do. They anticipate joint-marketing programs will enable them to generate more business from their existing clients, provide them opportunities to garner new clients and create better relationships with their current clients.

Providing Technical or Marketing Education

Education and support are other reasons to form relationships to have with an accounting or legal firm. Accountants and attorneys value education, and this education could be either technical or marketing in nature.

The needs of their clients are changing so rapidly that these professionals appreciate and value ways of staying up-to-date. Areas of technical information could include modern portfolio theory, tax-efficient investing and managing diversification (especially in closely-held corporate situations). Marketing education is also valued, and could include high-net-worth psychology, prospecting strategies and techniques of relationship management.

Depending on the situation, advisors provide these educational services in several ways. Often, they conduct an informal one-on-one meeting with the professional, and it may tie to a specific client situation or be general in nature. It's best to meet in their offices, as this gives you greater opportunity to meet more people and be more visible. Under certain circumstances, you may want to host a luncheon for several people in these firms.

Attorneys and accountants value education. This kind of education helps keep them keep up-to-date concerning the investment issues important to their clients. Moreover, marketing information and strategies make them more competitive.

Cross-Referral Arrangements

Cross-referrals sounds like a good idea, but are difficult to carry out in practice. It's unlikely that you and another professional can maintain an equal number of cross-referrals, or keep the caliber of these referrals the same. Experienced professionals will recognize this, and will avoid committing themselves to a large volume of referrals. On the other hand, if you generate a consistent referral stream to them, they will reciprocate.

Fee-Sharing or Other Compensation

Fee-splitting and other compensation arrangements should not be suggested to attorneys. Such arrangements are a violation of the ethical standards of the legal profession, and most attorneys are opposed to the practice.

Accountants, on the other hand, are open to such arrangements. Many states now allow accountants to accept fees, commissions and finder's fees so it is possible to share clients with accountants and to share fees for investment advisory services.

In developing your prospecting plan we recommend you focus on leveraging the client relationships you already have, as we discussed in the previous chapter.

Once this process in is place, turn your attention to building strategic alliances with a set of professional advisory firms to enhance your stream of new, wealthy prospects. The best targets for this program often are accounting firms and legal firms.

> ***"I've been rich and I've been poor. Rich is better."***
>
> ***- Frank Sinatra***

Then create a relationship development plan for each of these firms, focusing on why they should work with you. The choices include joint-marketing programs, education (technical and marketing), cross-referrals and compensation. The most effective of the four are are joint-marketing programs and education.

Producing Successful Seminars

Putting on seminars is a frequent component of joint-marketing programs with advisors (see the previous chapter) and on its own is generally the third most successful prospecting strategy. While your first priority should probably be leveraging your current client relationships for referrals and introductions, and your second should probably be developing strategic alliances with advisors, your third should probably be seminars.

The best seminars are a cross between a pedestrian college class and a high-energy vaudeville act. They take the best from each. From the college class, they take the educational process. From vaudeville acts they take the quality of showmanship. On a continuum between these two extremes,

> ***"Marketing is so basic that it cannot be considered a separate function. It is the whole business seen from the point of view of its final result, that is, from the customer's point of view... Business success is not determined by the producer but by the customer."***
>
> ***- Peter Drucker***

seminars fall somewhere in-between. Move too much towards one or the other of these two extremes, the seminar will fail — something we see all too often.

To assure your seminars are successful, you'll have to put in some effort. The affluent identify seminars as an excellent source of information. They readily attend seminars that they believe will provide them with useful information. The seminar must be perceived as adding real value if it's to attract and motivate wealthy investors.

Unfortunately, the responsiveness of the affluent to seminars has been noticed by many other investment advisors and financial services firms. Quite a few are marketing seminars these days. There is still room for anyone to be successful with seminars, however, if you follow the principles below.

Planning, Planning and More Planning

The key to the success of any effective seminar program is planning. A seminar is very much like a wedding. What makes a wedding a success is the vast amount of planning that makes the affair. In the same way, it is the planning that will determine if a seminar is a success or a failure.

Know Your Audience

The first thing you must do is decide who you want in your audience. Will they be mainly Family Stewards or Accumulators? In general terms, how wealthy will the audience be? Will you encourage people to bring spouses and families?

Your decisions about the composition of your audience will guide you in deciding what you will discuss and how you will present it. To make this decision, you have to begin with identifying just what you want to accomplish.

Your seminars have to be attuned to the audience. And, each audience is likely to be somewhat different requiring a different spin on the basic material.

One critical consideration when developing a seminar for the wealthy are the high-net-worth personalities of the attendees. You must gear what you say around their motivations to invest. Each personality will want to hear something that makes them believe you really understand them.

By understanding your audience you'll also know how to get the biggest bang for the buck. You'll know how to present your material to have the greatest impact.

The 2-to-1 Effort Rule

Abraham Lincoln explained that if he had eight hours to cut down a tree, he would spend the first six sharpening his ax. He felt the greatest success comes to those who make the most effort to prepare. This same logic holds true when it comes to putting on seminars.

The planning and preparation of the seminar should take twice as much effort as the follow-up. The remaining effort should be devoted to putting on the seminar. Therefore, 60% of the energy devoted to the seminar should be directed to the planning and preparation. The 60% should also include targeting the types of investors who would be interested in your topic. This is the "2" in the 2-to-1 Effort Rule.

The "1" is the follow-up. Thus, you should commit 30% of your effort to the follow-up. The personal meetings and follow-up sessions need to be geared to the needs of each individual investor.

Together, these two components of a seminar program—filling the seats and follow-up—account for 90% of your energies. This leaves 10% of the effort to be extended on the seminar itself. In putting on the seminar, focus on the quality of the presenters as well as the content.

Public Speaking

The inscription found in a 3,000-year-old Egyptian tomb reads, "Make thyself a craftsman in speech, for thereby thou shalt gain the upper hand." While your goals are to help others, not "gain the upper hand," it's clear that even 3,000 years ago, people recognized the power of an effective speaker. Then, as now, there are several principles to follow.

Grab and hold their attention. A fundamental principle of successful public speaking is to never be boring. You know that if a presenter is

boring, the speech is a failure. One mistake many financial advisors make is to lecture seminar participants on the technical aspects of their topic instead of relating to the people who are there. A useful discipline is to think of the high-net-worth personalities who will be there. If you imagine you are talking to a VIP or an Independent, you will automatically speak to their needs.

Organizing the presentation. To grab and hold the attention of your seminar participants means you have to organize the material in a way which captures their attention. Ensuring your presentations are well focused and structured, you will be most effective. When designing your talk, focus on a central theme. The central theme will act as a guide for arranging the material to make the presentation most persuasive. There are many ways to organize a presentation.

The most common organizational approach, because it is so very effective, is "state the case and prove it." The presentation begins with an introduction that establishes the central theme. Then supporting materials such as statistics, case examples, expert testimony, and the like are then used to support your theme. Finally, restate the central theme in your conclusion. In other words, start with the introduction ("Tell them what you are going to tell them"), then move through the body ("Tell them") and finally there is the conclusion ("Tell them what you told them").

Be passionate. Lyndon Johnson once said, "What convinces is conviction. Believe in the argument you're advancing. If you don't, you're as good as dead. The other person will sense something isn't there, and no chain of reasoning, no matter how logical or elegant or brilliant, will win your case for you."

As a presenter you can use passion to present your material convincingly. The material will not stand on its own, no matter how brilliant, accurate, timely or stimulating it is. The only way the material will take on a life of its own is if you present with passion and conviction.

It's fortunate that the key to motivating an audience is for you to sincerely believe in what you are saying. You wouldn't be in this business if you didn't believe in the benefits of professional investment management. You just need to communicate this conviction to each and every member of the audience.

When you present with passion and conviction, the audience will be convinced of your value. Affluent prospects should leave the presentation aware that it was valuable for them to hear you. The more they feel good about the talk, the more likely they will act. Your conviction helps create this sense of urgency.

A call to action. We must never lose sight of the reason seminars are put on. The only purpose of a seminar is to motivate the people in the audience to work with you. The presentation is always a call to action.

The seminar must inspire the audience. It must impel them to take the initiative and motivate them to want to come to you afterwards to discuss the ways you can be of service. Therefore, there must always be a "hook" built into your presentations. This way, once your wealthy audience is interested, they will want to seek you out to take the next step (which is to engage you to provide investment advisory services).

Investment Advisory Seminars

There are a wide variety of ways to put together investment advisory seminars. No one way is best. Results should be the only criteria for determining the effectiveness of one method over another.

As you begin to plan a seminar, consider a number critical planning variables: (1) the size of the audience; (2) the focus of the seminar; (3) handout materials; and (4) the use of guest presenters.

The size of the audience When it come to producing seminars for the affluent, you should limit the number of participants. It's usually a good idea to have "parlor meetings" instead of town-hall type get-togethers. It's most effective to create a small, intimate atmosphere, and well-orchestrated parlor meetings will create that effect.

The smaller surroundings of the meeting will also give you more opportunity to talk with individuals in the audience about the topic. It becomes less of a lecture and more of a dialogue.

The focus of the seminar. The best investment advisory seminars are about ways money management meets specific investor needs and wants. The best seminars do not focus on modern portfolio theory or specific investment products. The best seminars keep the money management function in the background.

What is in the foreground is high-net-worth psychology. You want to focus the seminar on the goals your audience is trying to achieve. For example, successful seminar topics for Family Stewards include how to plan for retirement, business succession planning and how to pay for college. VIPs are more interested in charitable giving while minimizing taxes is a good topic for Accumulators. With the focus of the seminar on investor goals, you will automatically avoid the highly technical discussions that are a turn-off to all investors instead of Gamblers and Innovators.

Handout materials. Attendees like to get something tangible at a seminar. If you provide handouts, you will help them focus on your presentation. Handout materials are also taken home to be re-read and provide an additional stimulus to action.

Using guest presenters. If you are involved in a joint-marketing situation (or if the topic calls for it) you'll be presenting along with someone else. Having several speakers is also more interesting for the audience.

Experts who complement your own areas of proficiency offer seminar participants a more interesting and involving experience. For example, if you are producing a seminar on private foundations you might focus on the benefits to the family and have an attorney explain some of the legal ramifications. Similarly, a guest presenter talking about the benefits of cross-tested plans for small business owners might be advisable. Guest presenters make sense when they add value.

> ***"Plans are nothing, planning is everything."***
> ***- Dwight D. Eisenhower***

One caveat is that having multiple speakers is more complicated to organize, and it's harder to insure the quality of each speaker. Put in the time to be sure you and your guest speakers are well prepared for the seminar. You want to work as a team toward achieving your shared goal of generating new business.

Seminars can significantly build your investment advisory business. Effective seminars require a great deal of planning. This planning should be focussed on the preparation of the seminar and on the follow-up after

the presentation. This is reflected in the 2-to-1 effort rule.

As for the presentation itself, a great deal hinges on your public speaking skills. You have to have a well-organized presentation which grabs and holds audience attention, and speak with passion and conviction.

You should keep the number of attendees limited when you conduct seminars with the affluent. Your handout materials should embody the central theme and the high points of your presentation. Outside presenters can augment the seminar.

III
Winning Affluent Investors

Positioning Asset Allocation

Asset allocation is a critical component of the construction of a portfolio for investment clients. It also provides a foundation and a framework for how you will interact with your clients. Because of this, asset allocation is a good way to provide value-added in terms of investment advisory services. Not only that, asset allocation is an invaluable tool in asset capture because it can give you a comprehensive overview of a client's entire portfolio as well as a compelling reason to bring the portfolio under single management (as we discuss in the chapter on asset capture).

In addition to these technical benefits, asset allocation is a powerful way to manage the expectations of your affluent clients. For this reason, we won't address asset allocation from a technical standpoint (you can find a lot of material on that elsewhere). Instead, we'll look at asset allocation as a way to win the business of wealthy investors.

> ***"You can be young without money, but you can't be old without it."***
> ***- Tennessee Williams***

Before continuing, take a moment and think about how you would explain your approach to asset allocation to a wealthy prospect you are meeting. How effective do you think your definition is in motivating that affluent investor to work with you?

Here are three ways we have heard investment advisors define asset allocation to wealthy prospects:

- "The distribution of the funds in a portfolio among asset classes such as equities, fixed-income securities and cash."
- "The systematic process of designing an optimal portfolio mix in accordance with specific risk and return parameters."
- "Creating an investment portfolio by diversifying into select asset classes so that the investment portfolio is properly situated on the efficient frontier."

Now, all these explanations are true in a technical sense; that is, these are three accurate definitions of asset allocation. Yet from the perspective of building a successful investment advisory business, how effective are these explanations in motivating prospects to work with you? For the most part, they're not.

How do you use explanations of asset allocation to motivate wealthy prospects to work with you? To truly motivate wealthy prospects (and succeed in well positioning asset allocation) you have to talk about financial concepts in ways clients understand.

High-net-worth psychology is the best way to accomplish this.

Taken as a group, affluent clients are generally at least somewhat aware of the concept of asset allocation, and most believe in its importance. However, when you look at affluent investors by their high-net-worth personalities, there are big differences in how important each type of high-net-worth personality thinks of asset allocation.

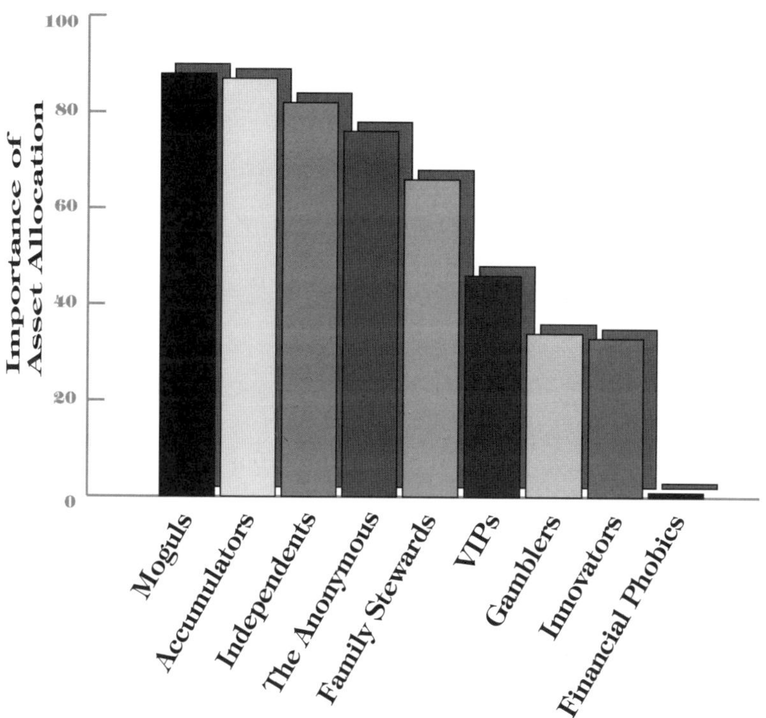

For example, Moguls (who are driven by control) are most likely to think asset allocation is very important (88%). So, too, are Accumulators (87%) because of their focus on returns. Many Independents (82%), Anonymous (76%) and Family Stewards (66%) agree that asset allocation is important. Several VIPs (46%) also are in accord.

You may wonder why so few of the most sophisticated segments—Gamblers (34%) and Innovators (33%)—think asset allocation is important. Think about their high-net-worth personalities. Because of their technical sophistication, these two personalities are not satisfied with the "basic" asset allocation models to which most investment advisors have access. To attract the interest of Gamblers and Innovators, the asset allocation models must incorporate the latest investment thinking.

Contrarily, it's obvious why Financial Phobics are at the bottom. They know too little to say that this (or any other) aspect of investing is important to them.

Which two or three high-net-worth personalities do most of your affluent clients posess? Take a minute to think about how you would position asset allocation to each of them. What will their responses be? How different is the high-net-worth psychology approach from what you use now?

This chapter will help you explain asset allocation to each of your current as well as potential wealthy clients based on high-net-worth psychology. The following table summarizes the various ways to position asset allocation to high-net-worth segments.

High-Net-Worth Personalities	***Primary Motivation***	***Positioning and Asset Allocation***
Family Stewards	Care of the Family	"I know your top priority is to **take care of your family.** Let me tell you about asset allocation, the best approach we know for managing your investments so you can be **comfortable knowing you have done the best job you can for your family."**
Financial Phobics	Avoid financial affairs	"I know **you don't like to get into long, technical discussions** about your investments, so I'll keep it short. Many of the best people in the industry have worried about figuring out what is the very best way to invest, it is asset allocation. If you give me the go-ahead, **I'm going to have a look at what you have got using this approach, and then we can talk again."**
Independents	Financial Freedom	"I'd like you to consider asset allocation. **Because your goal is to be financially independent** and flexible, I think asset allocation would be a good approach to explore. Asset allocation allows you to **directly relate your goals to the way your portfolio is invested."**

(continued) *High-Net-Worth Personalities*	*Primary Motivation*	*Positioning and Asset Allocation*
The Anonymous	Confiden-tiality, privacy	"I have been spending time thinking about your account. There is an approach called asset allocation I would like you to think about. I would like to prepare a **confidential** analysis for your review next time we meet."
Moguls	Power, control	"I know you like to **control** your portfolio, and an approach called asset allocation gives you the highest level of **control**. With asset allocation, you **set the overall strategy and make the major decisions."**
VIPs	Status, prestige	"Because your portfolio is an important one at this firm, we want to keep you current with the kinds of **investment approaches the leading investors are using.** The approach called asset allocation was proven by **modeling some of the largest pools of money in the country.** We think it's something you should consider given the importance of your portfolio."

(continued)

High-Net-Worth Personalities	*Primary Motivation*	*Positioning and Asset Allocation*
Accumulators	Asset Accumulation	"As you know, the very best way we know of today to **maximize your long-term investment performance** is asset allocation. Because your **number one objective is investment performance**, I think we should get into this a little more."
Gamblers	Thrill of investing	"I know **you have been reading** the materials on asset allocation I sent along. The reason I like it for you is that it's a way **of setting your aggressive risk profile** in the context of asset classes. It will also require rebalancing, so you will have to **stay involved."**
Innovators	New investment approaches	"Our **technical people have just added some state-of-the art** enhancements to our asset allocation approach I wanted you to know about first. These include..."

Family Stewards, you will recall, are affluent investors whose primary life motivation is to protect their family in every way possible, including financially. Family Stewards are often business owners and tend to keep a lot of assets in the business so the enterprise can provide employment for many family members. Family Stewards are very forward looking, and are as concerned about the education of their grandchildren as with helping children with down payments on their houses.

So how would you explain asset allocation to a Family Steward in a way that will motivate them to work with you? You might try something like, "I know your top priority is to take care of your family. Let me tell you about asset allocation, the best approach we know for managing your investments so you can be comfortable knowing you have done the best job you can for your family." The key is to link the idea of asset allocation to the core reason the wealthy client invests. When affluent investors hear you say you truly understand their goals, they are far more motivated to hear your recommendation.

The second largest affluent group is Financial Phobics. Financial Phobics dislike investing; they are scared and intimidated. For instance, they may be widows who have bequeathed the money after their husbands' deaths but they are overwhelmed by the responsibility. What they really want to do is pass along this responsibility to a trusted investment advisor. They don't want to learn, so you should not try to educate a Financial Phobic.

That said, how could you possibly explain asset allocation to a Financial Phobic? The short answer is that you don't. In the unlikely case they bring up the topic you should avoid all technical details. When you need to recommend this course of action, emphasize the advantages instead of the technical details by saying something like, "I know you don't like to get into long, technical discussions about your investments, so I'll keep it short. Many of the best people in the industry have worried about figuring out what is the very best way to invest, and they have come up with an approach called asset allocation. If you give me the go-ahead, I'm going to have a look at what you have got using this approach, and then we can talk again." Notice this approach avoids the specifics of what asset allocation is. However, it does provide reassurance and credibility by explaining how asset allocation has emerged as the current standard of excellence in portfolio management.

> ***"A wise man recognizes the convenience of a general statement, but he bows to the authority of a particular fact."***
> ***- Oliver Wendell Holmes***

Or, use an analogy, such as: "You have heard the saying don't put all your eggs in one basket. Asset allocation is basically this approach towards investing."

Not surprisingly, Independents seek personal independence. They dream about dropping everything and sailing off into the sunset. Their portfolios buy them personal autonomy, what they value above all.

How would you explain asset allocation to an Independent? How about something like, "I'd like you to consider asset allocation. Because your goal is to be financially independent and flexible, I think asset allocation would be a good approach to explore. Asset allocation allows you to directly relate your goals to the way your portfolio is invested." Independents have a modest understanding of investment concepts, so you can get into a little more detail, but stop short of too much technical information. If you can't tie what you are saying back to the goal of financial independence, forget it.

The Anonymous are a careful, closed group. They are fearful and worried about personal security and confidentiality. They need constant assurance that you are protecting the integrity of their information as well as their investments. How do you describe asset allocation to the Anonymous? Go light on technical explanations and emphasize how careful you are with information concerning their finances. You might try something like, "I have been spending time thinking about your account. There is an approach called asset allocation I would like you to think about. I would like to prepare a confidential analysis for your review next time we meet."

Moguls value money for the power it gives them. Power is all important to Moguls. They like to control people and environments around them. In working with Moguls, it's important that you and others in the firm treat them with the kind of deference and respect you give to people of power. Moguls are sensitive to the nuances of where people sit and how people are introduced. How would you position asset allocation to a Mogul? You would do so by emphasizing control, "I know you like to control your portfolio, and an approach called asset allocation gives you the highest level of control. With asset allocation, you set the overall strategy and make the major decisions."

VIPs are status oriented. They like to be recognized and acknowledged. They like prestigious surroundings and trophy possessions. How might you explain asset allocation to VIPs in terms they would recognize and to which they would relate? You could position asset allocation as the preferred investment approach of the rich and famous, "Because your portfolio is an important one at this firm, we want to keep you current with the kinds of investment approaches the leading investors are using. The approach called asset allocation was proven by modeling some of the largest pools of money in the country. We think it's something you should consider, given the importance of your portfolio."

Accumulators are more financially savvy than many other high-net-worth personalities, and are singularly focused on just one goal—accumulating more assets. As a result, they are the easiest group to whom you could explain asset allocation, "As you know, the very best way we know of today to maximize your long-term investment performance is asset allocation. Because your number one objective is investment performance, I think we should get into this a little more."

The last two groups (the smallest groups at 6% each) are the Gamblers and the Innovators. They are also, by far, the most knowledgeable and expert groups of all. Gamblers live, breathe and love investing. It is their hobby and often their life. Gamblers love the thrill of market volatility. They may know more about asset allocation than you do, "I know you have been reading the materials on asset allocation I sent along. The reason I like it for you is that it's a way of setting your aggressive risk profile in the context of asset classes. It will also require rebalancing, so you will have to stay involved."

Innovators are also extremely knowledgeable, but technically so. They like to be at the frontier of investment approaches—the cutting edge. They also may know more about asset allocation than most investment advisors, especially the technical aspects. They will be aware of the major theoretical debates surrounding asset allocation and will want to engage you in discussion. "Our technical people have just added some state-of-the-art enhancements to our asset allocation approach I wanted you to know about first. These include..."

If your goal is to motivate affluent investors to work with you, you will have noticed that the traditional, technical way of describing asset allocation has not been appropriate for any of the high-net-worth personalities. The traditional, technical way of talking about asset allocation just does not connect with the motivations and characteristics of affluent investors.

By putting the wealthy investor's needs and wants first, and by communicating that you understand these needs and wants, you can connect asset allocation to what is most important to your client. During the course of implementing asset allocation, you inevitably will need to present a more fact-based explanation of the process to your clients. The key is to use high-net-worth psychology to increase their desire to work with you.

Positioning Mutual Funds

For many investors, mutual funds comprise the bulk of their investment portfolios. Even among the wealthy, mutual funds play a very important role. Knowing how to position and sell mutual funds effectively is essential to success for investment advisors.

Traditionally, the benefits of mutual funds have been described to clients in ways such as:

- "Mutual funds are a good way of getting all the benefits of diversification."
- "With mutual funds, you will get professionals making the investment decisions."

Though these benefits are true the problem is that statements like the above do not motivate investors—especially affluent investors—to act. Why? Because they do not relate the benefits of mutual funds to the core wants and needs of investors.

"I don't like money, actually, but it quiets my nerves."

- Joe Louis

You will be more effective getting prospects and clients to act on your recommendations if you show you really understand their

needs, wants, feeling, desires and so forth. To motivate clients you have to talk about financial concepts in ways to which they readily relate.

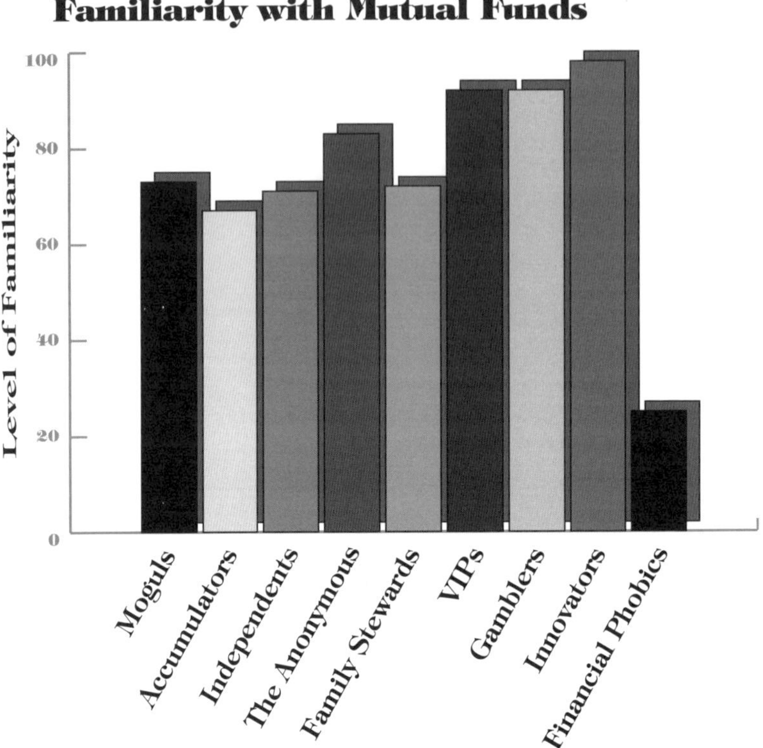

Just about all the high-net-worth personalities (with the exception, of course, of the Financial Phobics) are pretty familiar with mutual funds. They could have bought them, or just feel they know what they are enough to make a decision about them. Three quarters or more of the Innovators (98%), VIPs (92%), Gamblers (92%) and the Anonymous (83%) are very familiar with mutual funds, as are almost as many Moguls (73%), Family Stewards (72%), Independents (71%) and

Accumulators (67%). Only Financial Phobics say they are not very familiar with mutual funds (25%).

If your clients are like these types and are already very familiar with mutual funds, how can you motivate them to further consider such an investment? How well have you positioned mutual funds amid the goals of your top clients? Most importantly, thinking of your top clients as high-net-worth personalities; how could you make a stronger case for using mutual funds?

Positioning Mutual Funds Using High-Net-Worth Psychology

This chapter will help you explain mutual funds to your clients based on high-net-worth psychology. The table below summarizes the assorted ways to position mutual funds to the various high-net-worth personalities.

High-Net-Worth Personalities	***Primary Motivation***	***Positioning Mutual Funds***
Family Stewards	Care of the Family	"From everything you have told me, I know **your number one goal is to take care of your family.** I think these funds are the best way we can achieve your goal of **safeguarding your family** as you manage your investments."

(continued) ***High-Net-Worth Personalities***	***Primary Motivation***	***Positioning Mutual Funds***
Financial Phobics	Avoid financial affairs	"I'm glad **we had the time to get caught up.** Your trip sounded great. Let me **quickly turn to business for a moment.** This sheet lists the most important feature of the three funds I mentioned last time. Let's **have a little look** at these."
Independents	Financial Freedom	"Because you want nothing more than to **be financially independent and flexible,** I think you should explore how certain mutual funds might help you get there. These funds will **help get you out of the corporate rat race early."**
The Anonymous	Confidentiality, privacy	**"Let me close the door.** OK, I **privately have prepared** this overview of some mutual funds I think you should look at."
Moguls	Power, control	"Let's get **control** over this portfolio. Incorporating these mutual funds will **enable you to implement** your strategy. You now have some **major decisions to make."**
VIPs	Status, prestige	"I know you have your eye on that condo in that **Florida gated community. Doesn't someone famous live there?**...Why don't we take a good look at these mutual funds. **The portfolio manager for this one, for example, was just profiled in..."**

(continued) ***High-Net-Worth Personalities***	***Primary Motivation***	***Positioning Mutual Funds***
Accumulators	Asset Accumulation	"Your priority is **investment performance**. You want to **maximize your long-term investment performance.** I've analyzed the **investment performance** of a wide variety of funds, and want to go over these **numbers** with you."
Gamblers	Thrill of investing	"I wouldn't bring up these funds for everyone, **but I know you understand this sort of specialized fund.** These carry more risk, but could play a role in your portfolio. Let's go over the details; I know you like to **dig into the facts."**
Innovators	New investment approaches	"I know you like **break-throughs in investment** theory. We have **new research** that shows that there is a new vector we should consider in our approach to portfolio selection. Let me share the **analysis** with you, and go over a new fund we have that is **built around this principle."**

The largest segment is Family Stewards, and they are motivated by their need to protect their family in every way possible, including financially. Often business owners, Family Stewards are accustomed to planning their business and personal financial decisions around the needs of their families. For example, the business often accommodates family members who need employment and provides financing to others. Family Stewards take a multi-generational approach and worry a lot about the well-being of children and grandchildren.

In planning how to explain mutual funds to Family Stewards you need to remember their basic motivations. Think about ways you can tie your recommendation of mutual funds to their focus on the family. You might try something like, "From everything you have told me, I know your number one goal is to take care of your family. I think these funds are the best way we can achieve your goal of safeguarding your family as you manage your investments." The important thing is to relate the idea of mutual funds to the core reason the wealthy client invests. When affluent investors know you truly understand their objective they are far more motivated to hear your investment ideas.

Financial Phobics comprise a large and profitable group of affluent investors. They're among the most loyal of clients once you have won their trust. However, winning their trust is an uphill task. The key is to recognize that Financial Phobics really, truly dislike investing. Financial Phobics are fearful of investing and suspicious of investment advisors. They avoid financial discussions; they are scared of them and are easily intimidated. They often feel overwhelmed by the idea of making investment decisions. They would vastly prefer to give the responsibility to a trusted investment advisor.

The difficulty is how you could possibly explain mutual funds to Financial Phobics, given that they want to avoid any technical discussions. You should shift to talking about advantages of mutual funds in a way Financial Phobics can understand. You could say something like, "I'm glad we had the time to get caught up. Your trip sounded great. Let me quickly turn to business for a moment. This sheet lists the most important features of the three funds I mentioned last time. Let's have a little look at these." In this instance, the investment advisor first had a good discussion with the client about personal matters, such as her trip. Only after the client was relaxed did the investment advisor shift to business. Notice the investment advisor simplified the choices for the wealthy client by showing a few funds and just the most salient features of each. He provided comprehensive data in a folder. This approach avoids the technical discussions Financial Phobics dislike while providing reassurance.

Independents prize personal and financial independence above all. They dream of long trips and few responsibilities. They have figured out that investing is their means to that end. Good investing will create the personal and financial freedom they crave. Given this strong motivation, how would you explain mutual funds to an Independent? How about something like, "Because you want nothing more than to be financially independent and flexible, I think you should explore how certain mutual funds might help you get there. These funds will help get you out of the corporate rat race early." Compared to some other affluent investors, Independents are not all that sophisticated about investing. They know a few things about investing, so you can get into a little more detail, but you should not provide too much technical information. A good rule to follow is if you can't tie what you are saying back to the goal of financial independence, forget it.

"It is useless to tell a river to stop running; the best thing is to learn how to swim in the direction it is flowing."
- Anonymous

The distinguishing characteristic of the Anonymous is their need for privacy and confidentiality. They worry a lot, and are fearful. They need constant reassurance that their investment advisors are relentless in protecting the integrity of their information as well as overseeing their investments.

The Anonymous are average in their understanding of investments. Given all this, how should you position mutual funds to the Anonymous? You primarily should emphasize how careful you are with information concerning their finances. Try something like, "Let me close the door. OK, I privately have prepared this overview of some mutual funds I think you should look at." Notice that the investment advisor is careful to point out how careful he is to preserve the privacy of the conversation when he closes the door.

Moguls comprise the group most concerned about power and personal influence. They value money for the power it gives them. Moguls have a high need to control the people and places around them. When you work with Moguls, you should be careful to treat them with the kind of deference and respect you typically give to people of power. Moguls pay attention to the small power gestures and courtesies. With this understanding, how would you position mutual funds to a Mogul? You effectively position mutual funds by emphasizing control, "Lets get control over this portfolio. Incorporating these mutual funds will enable you to implement your strategy. You now have some major decisions to make."

VIPs love prestige. They are status oriented. They like to be recognized and acknowledged. VIPs value prestigious surroundings and trophy possessions. Given this value system, how could you explain mutual funds to a VIP in terms VIPs would recognize and relate to? For VIPs, you should position mutual funds as the preferred investment approach of the rich and famous: "I know you have your eye on that condo in that Florida gated community. Doesn't someone famous live there? ... Why don't we take a good look at these mutual funds. The portfolio manager for this one, for example, was just profiled in..."

Accumulators are one of the more financially sophisticated high-net-worth personalities. They also are the group most likely to be fixated on investment performance. That's because they are focused on the sole goal of accumulating more assets. As a result, they are the easiest group to whom you will explain any investment product, as long as you concentrate on investment performance. You might position mutual funds to an Accumulator in this way, "Your priority is investment performance. You want to maximize your long-term investment performance. I've analyzed the investment performance of a wide variety of funds, and want to go over these numbers with you."

Gamblers are extremely involved in investing. They are sophisticated and knowledgeable. Gamblers enjoy every facet of investing, probe into details and read extensively. Gamblers are distinguished by their higher risk profile and their search for the hot investment. How would you position mutual funds to a Gambler? You should show them how these investments fit into their portfolio: "I wouldn't bring up these funds to everyone, but I know you understand this sort of specialized fund. These carry more risk, but could play a role in your portfolio. Let's go over the details; I know you like to dig into the facts."

Innovators are also extremely sophisticated and knowledgeable.

Unlike Gamblers, though, they are more interested in technical matters. Innovators like to be at the cutting edge. In general, they know a lot about financial products such as mutual funds, especially the technical aspects. Innovators will be aware of the major issues involved in mutual fund and investing. They especially like learning something new "I know you like breakthroughs in investment theory. We have new research that shows that there is a new vector we should consider in our approach to portfolio selection. Let me share the analysis with you, and go over a new fund we have that is built around this principle."

When you position mutual funds, you can relate your recommendations to the high-net-worth psychology of the affluent investor. If you are like other investment advisors who have adopted this system, you will find your clients are more receptive to your recommendations. Put the affluent investor's need first and connect that need to mutual funds. Do this and you'll be more effective in motivating them to work with you.

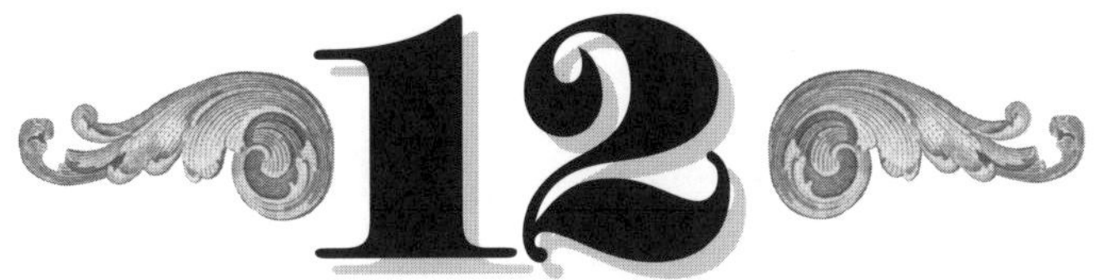

12

Positioning Managed Accounts

Do you want to shrink your managed account sales cycle by 40%? Do you want to grow your fee-based consulting business by 52%? Do you want to generate four times more referrals for managed accounts?

> ***"Money is a terrible master but an excellent servant."***
> ***—Phineas T. Barnum***

Results like these are possible by staying focussed on what's important to your managed accounts clients and prospects. Investment advisors who have already started using high-net-worth psychology are seeing results like these.

High-net-worth psychology guides you in explaining managed accounts to wealthy prospects and shows you how to reinforce the value of managed accounts to current, affluent clients. By consistently using high-net-worth psychology, you should be able to shorten your managed account sales cycle, grow your fee-based business and generate more managed account referrals than ever before.

Affluent investors are increasingly interested in managed accounts.

Ask Moguls whether or not they are interested in managed accounts and 96% will say yes. Also giving the nod are VIPs (95%), Financial Phobics (93%), Family Stewards (91%), Accumulators (90%) and the Anonymous (89%). Independents are only slightly less interested (74%). The two exceptions to this very high level of interest are Gamblers (24%) and Innovators (17%). Despite fewer being interested in managed accounts, there are still good prospects among Gamblers and Innovators.

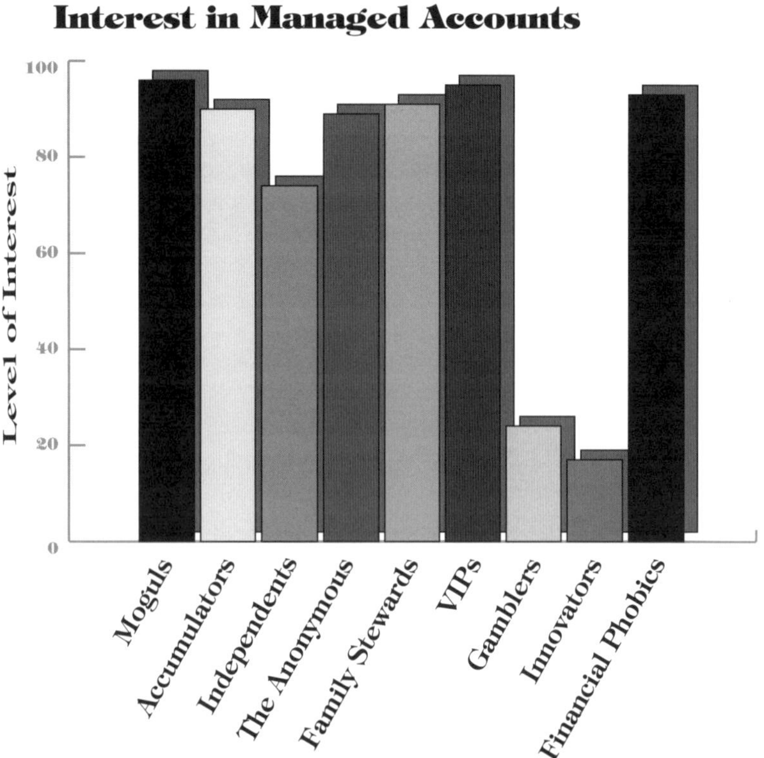

Before reading ahead, stop to think for a minute. What high-net-worth personalities are most represented among your managed account clients? Are they Family Stewards or Accumulators? Now think back to exactly what it was about managed accounts that was the hot button for each of your clients (using high-net-worth psychology).

The key to using high-net-worth psychology is to always remember that not all investors are alike. Each of the nine personalities is interested in managed accounts for a different reason. Use the right reason with the appropriate clients or prospects, and it is easier to sell them managed accounts.

High-Net-Worth Personalities	***Primary Motivation***	***Positioning Managed Accounts***
Family Stewards	Care of the Family	"A managed account fits your situation because you will be able to **take care of your family's financial future."**
Financial Phobics	Avoid financial affairs	"Many of my clients prefer managed accounts because they can **confidently leave investment decision chores** to experienced money managers with proven track records."
Independents	Financial Freedom	"A managed account is the best approach for you because you want **financial independence."**
The Anonymous	Confidentiality, privacy	"You should seriously consider managed accounts because we are able to ensure the higest level of **confidentiality and privacy."**

(continued) High-Net-Worth Personalities	Primary Motivation	Positioning Managed Accounts
Moguls	Power, control	"Managed accounts are a good choice because you have the **power** to set strategy and **be in charge** of your portfolio."
VIPs	Status, prestige	"A managed account will suit your needs because we can bring all our expertise to bear on your **personal** account and give it the **attention it deserves."**
Accumulators	Asset Accumulation	"A managed account fits your situation because you will be able to **accumulate assets** rapidly."
Gamblers	Thrill of investing	"A managed account suits your risk profile because you can **determine the amount of risk** you want at any given time."
Innovators	New investment approaches	"I think you'll like this managed account program because you'll be able to access **cutting-edge** money managers."

The key is to concentrate on what is important about managed accounts based on the specific high-net-worth personality of the affluent investor. Let's look at each of the nine high-net-worth personalities and discuss how this is done.

The appeal of managed accounts to Family Stewards is that they

can be used to safeguard their investments for their family. Family Stewards want first and foremost to take care of their family. To a Family Steward you might say: "A managed account fits your situation because you will be able to take care of your family's financial future."

Periodic investment reviews and prescreened managers are big selling points to Family Stewards. In relaying a selling point to a Family Steward you can say, "You'll be able to obtain the best possible care for your family's portfolio because you can choose among prescreened investment managers. And, with our frequent updates and periodic investment reviews, you will be able to keep tabs on your progress in reaching your financial goals for your family."

Financial Phobics are interested in managed accounts because after making the big decisions—to use a managed account and the selection of the investment management consultant—they can withdraw from involvement. Financial Phobics are not interested in investment decision-making and often are fearful and risk adverse. You could effectively position managed accounts to a Financial Phobic by saying, "Many of my clients prefer managed accounts because they can confidently leave investment decision chores to experienced money managers with proven track records."

Remember to connect features to the reassurances Financial Phobics seek. Financial Phobics value a consultant's recommend-

ation. Therefore, you might say, "It's hard, when you're not an expert, to pick money managers. That's why I recommend managed accounts because we can use experts to select money managers and then you won't need to worry any more. You'll feel comfortable knowing you made the best possible choice."

Independents are attracted to managed accounts because they provide the freedom to set their own objectives and investment style. Moreover, Independents readily understand that managed accounts are a pathway to achieving the financial independence they desire. To an Independent you might say, "A managed account is the best approach for you because you want financial independence." For an Independent, a statement like this is straight to the point.

A big selling point for Independents is to be able to select money managers with complementary investment styles. You can communicate this by saying, "Managed accounts are a good way for you to achieve your objective because you will be able to choose from money managers who complement each other and who will work towards your goal of financial independence." It's important to always relate every feature to the core goal of the Independent—personal financial freedom.

The Anonymous focus on privacy. They like to play their cards close to their chests. To an Anonymous you might say, "You should seriously consider managed accounts because we are able to ensure the highest level of confidentiality and privacy."

For the Anonymous, a motivator is the ability to establish a long-term relationship. An effective positioning for an Anonymous might be, "Managed accounts fit your goals because you will quietly and privately be able to manage your investments. Because I am going to be here to help you, you will always be able to control the information about your financial affairs."

Moguls like managed accounts because they can be in charge and Moguls can increase their feeling of control and power over their affairs if they use managed accounts. To position managed accounts you need to communicate these motivations to Moguls. For example, during the presentation you might say, "Managed accounts are a good choice because you have the power to set strategy and be in charge of your portfolio."

As you describe the various features of managed accounts to a Mogul, it's important to relate each feature back to the core benefits of managed accounts. For example, you should emphasize to Moguls that they will be in control because they can access top managers and have the ability to easily change managers. When positioning managed accounts to a Mogul, you might say, "A managed account program is a really good fit for your needs because you have the power to change money managers whenever you think necessary. You also can access the very top money managers in the investment advisory world, people you couldn't have working for you any other way."

VIPs are attracted to managed accounts because of their privileged image (managed accounts are the choice of large firms and wealthy investors). Recall that VIPs seek status, prestige and the respect and deference of others. You can position a managed account to a VIP by saying, "A managed account will suit your needs because we can bring all of our expertise to bear on your personal account and give it the attention it deserves."

Remember to tie every feature of managed accounts back to the status and prestige needs of VIPs. Big selling points for VIPs are periodic investment reviews, asset allocation and the consultant's recommendation. Thus, you might say to a VIP, "I recommend a managed account because we will schedule full-blown periodic investment review sessions. For an account of this importance, we will want to bring in our best people and most thorough research."

Accumulators like managed accounts because they can use the service to plan their returns. Also, they like the idea of carefully tracking their investments. So you might say to an Accumulator, "A managed account fits your situation because you will be able to accumulate assets rapidly." As with the Independent, this statement is direct.

An important factor for Accumulators is the single fee. Thus, you can say, "One of the features of a managed account program you will like is the single fee. This is because your returns won't be affected by hidden fees and charges so you will be able to maximize your returns and build up that capital position. " Again, it's important to tie the features of managed accounts directly back to the high-net-worth personality with whom you are dealing.

Although Gamblers like to manage portions of their portfolio personally, many are interested in managed accounts for their core portfolio strategies. A principal attraction of managed accounts is the ability for Gamblers to set their own risk levels. You could bring this out by saying something like, "A managed account suits your risk profile because you can determine the amount of risk you want at any given time."

For Gamblers a big selling point is access to aggressive top money managers. You could bring this feature home by pointing out, "Because of your aggressive investment style, with a managed account you can use the services of some of the biggest hitting money managers."

About one quarter of Innovators are attracted to managed accounts because this high-net-worth personality is interested in access to sophisticated expertise. You can show you understand this by mentioning something like, "I think you'll like this managed account program because you'll be able to access cutting-edge money managers."

A big selling point for Innovators is access to leading investment styles and products. To make a big selling point in the conversation you might say, "You'll like this managed account because you will be able to use the services of some of the most sophisticated and innovative money managers in the world, portfolio managers you otherwise would be unable to get."

The most successful investment advisors using high-net-worth psychology started simply and deliberately. Before meeting with a managed account prospect, they would compose a list of the points they wanted to make about managed accounts down one side of the page. Opposite each point, they would write some phrases they could use to relate that feature back to the basic need of the personality, just as we have portrayed in the examples in this chapter. Some have gone to the trouble of writing scripts to engender this way of selling as second nature.

"There is an old saying in Spain.
To be a bullfighter,
you must first learn to be a bull."
- Anonymous

At one of our recent workshops, we were explaining how to use high-net-worth psychology in positioning managed accounts, and Sam brought up this example, "You know, that makes me remember the time I called on a woman who I now know is a clear Financial Phobic. I just went in with my usual canned pitch. As we left, I said to myself I'll never see that account.' Now I know what I should have done. I should have downplayed the nuts-and-bolts of the program—big time. I should have brought the presentation, but only as a leave-behind. And I should have had a lot of reassuring things to say and stories to tell."

13

Positioning Alternative Investments

Alternative investments include a variety of investment vehicles such as private equity and hedge funds. For affluent investors, alternative investments are an increasingly important component of their investment portfolios. Investors are attracted by the historically high returns of these investment vehicles as well as their fit in a portfolio as some are designed to be uncorrelated to traditional investment vehicles.

Alternative investments raise several issues for investment advisors. One is how to determine which affluent investors are appropriate for these investments. Another is how to best position alternative investments to wealthy investors. It's your job as an investment advisor to determine suitability. You have to determine if, for example, hedge funds are the most appropriate investment vehicle

> ***"If little kids don't aspire to make money like I did, what the hell good is this country?"***
>
> ***- Lee Iacocca***

and then, if so, which hedge funds. Once you have determined suitability, use high-net-worth psychology to effectively position alternative investments to your wealthy clients.

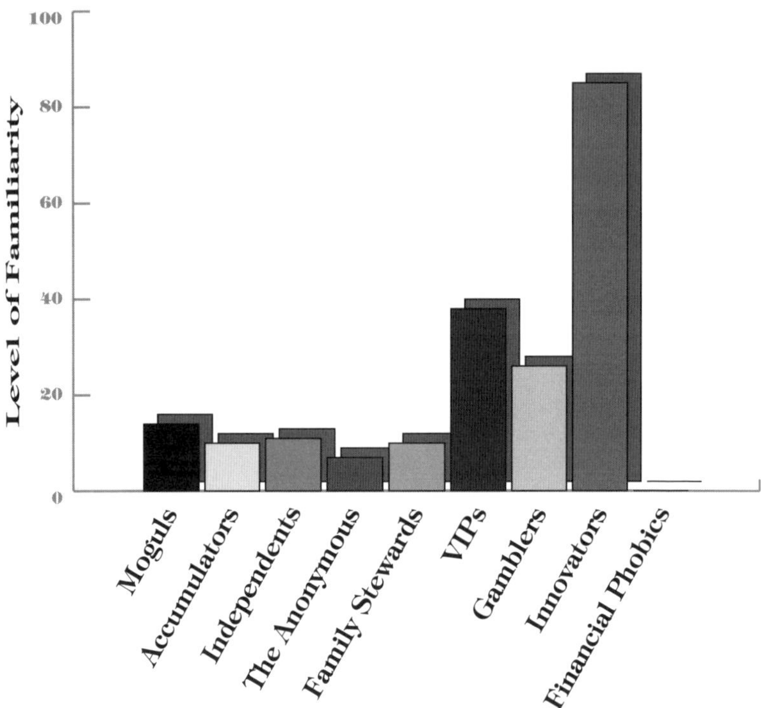

Affluent investors vary widely in the extent to which they are familiar with alternative investments. As the table shows, almost all Innovators (85%) are very familiar with private equity. We would expect this, given their passionate interest in innovative investments. Most every other kind of high-net-worth personality is unfamiliar with private equity as an individual investment option. Note that not one of the Financial Phobics says that they are very familiar with private investments—again, as we would expect given this category's high-net-worth personality.

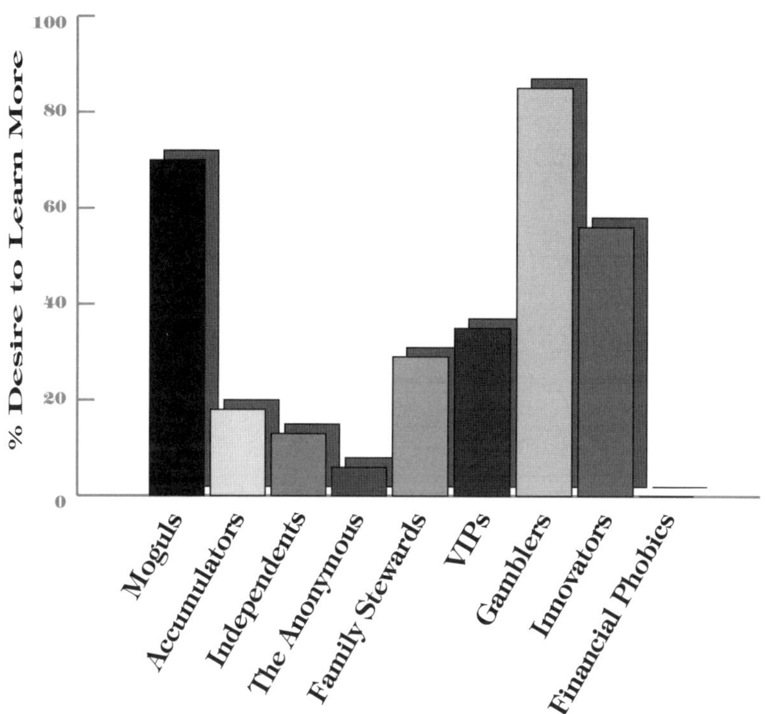

Investment advisors also need to be aware of wealthy investors who need more information about alternative investments. Affluent investors who already are familiar (like Innovators usually are) do not need much more information; that's why just 56% of Innovators say they would like more information. Some of the other personalities who tend not to stray from the tried-and-true in investment strategy

(Financial Phobics and the Anonymous) don't want to know anything about hedge funds, as the table shows. Gamblers (85%) and Moguls (70%) are highly motivated to learn more; hedge funds appeal to their basic investment motivations, as we will see later. Other high-net-worth personalities—VIPs (35%), Family Stewards (29%), Accumulators (18%) and Independents (13%) — approach alternative investments with interest, but cautiously.

How can you know who is already familiar with alternative investments and who wants to learn more? How can you know how to position alternative investments with each type of investor? High-net-worth psychology is the most effective approach.

You probably already have an instinctive sense of how your top wealthy clients respond to alternative investments. But now think of them in terms of their high-net-worth personalities. Which of these wealthy clients should you approach with these products and how should you position those investment opportunities?

This chapter will help you explain alternative investments to various clients based on their high-net-worth psychology. A summary is provided in the following table.

High-Net-Worth Personalities	***Primary Motivation***	***Positioning Alternate Investments***
Family Stewards	Care of the Family	"We both know your top priority is to **take care of your family.** That means a careful approach to investing. However we might want to evaluate these investments because used in the right way they could round out your portfolio and give you the benefit of further diversification which will **safeguard your family in the long term."**
Financial Phobics	Avoid financial affairs	"That's a great story. Listen, **I know you don't like to get into the details** of investing, but there are some opportunities I'd **like to touch on** with you."
Independents	Financial Freedom	"I think we should explore how certain hedge funds might help you **achieve your goal of financial independence.** These products are complex, but might balance out you portfolio and help you achieve your **objective of independence."**
The Anonymous	Confidentiality, privacy	"Now that **we are alone,** let's go over this **confidential review** of your position. Now, let's look ahead. We have some **private investment opportunities** you might want to consider."

(continued) **High-Net-Worth Personalities**	***Primary Motivation***	***Positioning Alternate Investments***
Moguls	Power, control	"You've got a very **powerful position** here. Have you ever considered the **power and leverage** in investments such as hedge funds or private equity? These could be some **major decision points** for you."
VIPs	Status, prestige	"You know how **exclusive** hedge funds are, and how **participation is so restricted.** We have some exciting opportunities **I can't bring to just anybody."**
Accumulators	Asset Accumulation	"Since your **priority is return**, you should look at how these investments might boost your overall **investment performance.** I've modeled the impact some of these might have on your overall return. I know your goal is to **maximize your long-term investment performance."**
Gamblers	Thrill of investing	**"I just uncovered some very interesting opportunities.** They **aren't for everybody** because of the **risk**, but I **thought of you immediately, because you understand** these things. I'm **faxing over some top line material, but let me let you in on..."**
Innovators	New investment approaches	"We've got some **new private equity opportunities** I wanted you to be the **first to know about.** They have some interesting aspects that are **pretty novel.** Let me tell you **what's unique."**

Family Stewards, as you know very well by now, tend to be more cautious and conservative than some of the other personalities. Because they are very interested in taking care of their families, many of them will want to know about alternative investments. They will trust you to help them sort out the options because you understand their attitudes and values so thoroughly.

When you consider exactly how to explain alternative investments to a Family Steward, you should start with their basic motivations. You might try something like, "We both know your top priority is to take care of your family. That means a careful approach to investing. However, we might want to evaluate these investments because used in the right way they could round out your portfolio and give you the benefit of further diversification which will safeguard your family in the long term."

You may want to think twice before thinking about positioning alternative investments to a Financial Phobic. They don't know much about investing and are resistant to learning anything more. They are very conservative and risk adverse. However, you may find yourself in the position of wanting to recommend an alternative investment to a Financial Phobic because of one's specific situation. In this case, consider something like, "That's a great story. Listen, I know you don't like to get into the details of investing, but there are some opportunities I'd like to touch on with you." The investment advisor in this instance took the time to talk about personal matters with the client, and only when they got caught up did he bring up investments. He planned out a short and simple overview and left materials to be read later.

Independents may be good candidates for alternative investments as their goals (personal and financial independence) will usually require well-diversified portfolios. On the other hand, they are not among the most financially sophisticated of the nine high-net-worth personalities. Given this background, how would you explain alternative investments to an Independent? How about something like, "I think we should explore how certain hedge funds might help you achieve your goal of financial independence. These products are complex, but might balance out your portfolio and help you achieve your objective of independence."

"You never really understand a person until you consider things from their point of view — until you climb into their skin and walk around in it."
- Harper Lee

The privacy and confidentiality needs so characteristic of the Anonymous can provide you a point of leverage for positioning alternative products. Your approach will have to take into account that they worry a lot, are average in their sophistication and are generally fearful. They will need your reassurance and support in evaluating these investment options.

What is the best way to position alternative investments to the Anonymous? As always, begin by reinforcing how careful you are with information about their financial affairs. Try something like, "Now that we are alone, let's go over this confidential review of your position. Now, let's look ahead. We have some private investment opportunities you might want to consider."

Because they have the high-net-worth personality most concerned about power and personal influence, Moguls are a natural candidate for alternative investments. Moguls value money for the power it gives them, and would find much of interest to them in private equity investments and hedge funds.

With this understanding, how would you position alternative investments to a Mogul? You effectively position private equity and hedge funds as you do all other investment opportunities — by emphasizing control: "You've got a very powerful position here. Have you ever considered the power and leverage in investments such as hedge funds or private equity? These could be some major decision points for you."

Because VIPs love prestige and status, alternative investments give them an opportunity to add to their prestigious possessions, because hedge funds and private equity have an aura of exclusivity.

Given this value system, how could you explain alternative investments to a VIP in their terms? For VIPs, you should position alternative investments as the preferred investment approach among the elite: "You know how exclusive hedge funds are, and how participation is so restricted. We have some exciting opportunities I can't bring to just anybody."

Because Accumulators are one of the most financially sophisticated groups of investors, you can expect a fair amount of familiarity with alternative investments. Because they are the most fixated on investment performance, they will be highly interested in alternative investments.

Because of these factors, they're one of the easiest personalities to whom you can explain alternative investment products, as long as you keep bringing the discussion back to investment performance. You might position alternative investments to an Accumulator in this way, "Since your priority is return, you should look at how these investments might boost your overall investment performance. I've modeled the impact some of these might have on your overall return. I know your goal is to maximize your long-term investment performance."

Gamblers are instantly attracted to alternative investments because of their risk profile. Gamblers are sophisticated and knowledgeable enough to generally understand what they are getting into. Because Gamblers always are interested in today's hot investment, hedge funds and private equity opportunities are compelling. It does not take much to position alternative investments to a Gambler, "I just uncovered some very interesting opportunities. They aren't for everybody because of the risk, but I thought of you immediately, because you understand these things. I'm faxing over some top line material, but let me let you in on..."

Like Gamblers, Innovators are financially sophisticated and knowledgeable. Unlike Gamblers, however, they are more interested in the technical details and state-of-the-art approaches. In talking with Innovators you need to keep in mind that they like to be at the cutting-edge of investment technology. In the area of alternative investments, they will be the most knowledgeable of any segment, so you should shift quickly to the specifics: "We've got some new private equity opportunities I wanted you to be the first to know about. They have some interesting aspects that are pretty novel. Let me tell you what's unique."

All high-net-worth personalities potentially are clients for any type of investment depending on their particular situations. However, our analysis shows that each type shares some general characteristics when it comes certain to alternative investments—hedge funds and private equity.

Some high-net-worth personalities will be more or less familiar with the product. Some high-net-worth personalities will be more or less ready to relate to alternative investments on the basis of their risk profile. And some high-net-worth personalities will be more or less interested in working with you in this area. All of which exemplify the reason to put the wealthy investor's needs and wants first and connect them to alternative investment opportunities.

Positioning Retirement and Estate Planning

Retirement and estate planning have gained tremendous new importance for primarily two reasons. First, the average age of investors is creeping upwards. As the Baby Boom generation enters their 50s, retirement and estate planning are becoming major concerns. Investment advisors accustomed to consulting only on investments are now increasingly being called upon to answer questions about estate and retirement planning.

The second reason for the rise in importance of retirement and estate planning is the interest in grabbing a larger share of the wallet. Like asset allocation and charitable planning, these planning tools can provide an investment advisor with a comprehensive overview of an investor's portfolio and asset structure. Because most wealthy investors divide their portfolios among three or more investment advisors, it can

> ***"Put not your trust in money, but put your money in trust."***
> ***- Oliver Wendell Holmes***

be difficult for you to determine that which you are not managing unless you do some sort of comprehensive planning for the client (see Chapter 17).

To meet client planning needs, many financial institutions have created packages for investment advisors when working with a client on retirement and investment planning. These packages range from software installed on the investment advisor's PC to elaborate customized binders an investment advisor can give to a client.

As they grow older, more and more affluent investors are finding that retirement and estate planning are important to them, particularly because of the marketing efforts of financial institutions. Three segments already are well aware of the benefits of retirement and estate planning; Accumulators (82%), the Anonymous (75%) and Family Stewards (72%).

About one-quarter of several other segments is beginning to believe in the importance of retirement and estate panning, but others rapidly are becoming more motivated. Currently, Financial Phobics (26%), Independents (24%) and VIPs (20%) constitute a strong growing market for retirement and planning services. However, there are three segments you will have to persuade and motivate. Innovators (14%) and Gamblers (13%) are so focused on the here and now of investing, it takes a little more effort to refocus them on certain types of future planning. Moguls are a high potential segment as just 3% believe retirement and estate planning are important, and yet such planning can meet their control needs.

Importance of Retirement & Estate Planning

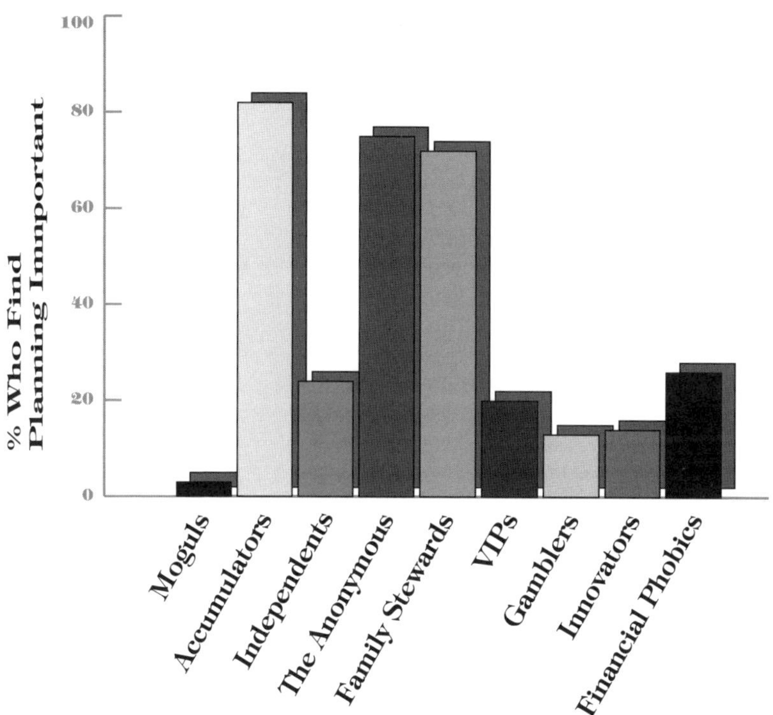

Despite substantial awareness of the importance of retirement and estate planning among many of the affluent, it still is easy to poorly position these services without the benefit of high-net-worth psychology. Investment advisors can make the mistake of focusing on aspects of planning that have no relevance to the wealthy individual and therefore lose the opportunity for building the relationship, not to

mention assets under management. We have seen investment advisors explain the benefits of retirement and estate planning to clients these ways:

- "Now is the time to think about your retirement. I just need a little information. First of all, how much income will you need when you retire?
- "We need to do a systematic analysis of your estate tax position, and evaluate the use of various trusts in order to convey those assets."
- "We have brought out a new, comprehensive planning service for estate and retirement planning. When we finish the process, you will have a plan like this (show binder)."

Depending on the wealthy investor, these statements may provide some motivation, but clearly this motivation is not compelling. Compelling motivation is a call to action delivered in ways that are impossible for clients to ignore. The key to delivering an effective call to action is high-net-worth psychology.

Now let's use high-net-worth psychology to explain retirement and estate planning to various clients. The table below summarizes the various ways to position retirement and estate planning to high-net-worth personalities.

Using High-Net-Worth Psychology to Position Retirement and Estate Planning Services

High-Net-Worth Personalities	***Primary Motivation***	***Positioning Retirement & Estate Planning Services***
Family Stewards	Care of the Family	"Since **taking care of family** is so important to you, I think we should look at estate planning in the light of some new ways we can use to **protect your loved ones.**"
Financial Phobics	Avoid financial affairs	"I know you get a little **frustrated around money,** but I think if you know exactly where you are, you will **definitely be able to relax.** Let me do a retirement analysis for you. I'm almost certain you will see that you will be very well off for the rest of your days, and you should **start thinking about what you would like to do with your time.**"
Independents	Financial Freedom	"You want nothing more than to **do what you want to do, when you want to do it.** I think you are just at the point of being **independent,** but let's update your retirement plan just to be sure."

(continued) ***High-Net-Worth Personalities***	***Primary Motivation***	***Positioning Retirement & Estate Planning Services***
The Anonymous	Confiden-tiality, privacy	"I know how important the **confidentiality** of your financial information is to you. To keep things as **private as possible,** we need to do an estate plan. I have software right here in my PC that will let me do the job, so your **data will never leave this office** until it's time to talk to a lawyer."
Moguls	Power, control	"You've told me how you have **had to stay on top** of your kids because you're not sure how they will handle wealth. If we get on top of that estate planning now, we can **set up the kind of good controls** you want."
VIPs	Status, prestige	"You're going to want to have the **finer things and the rewards** of life when you retire. Let's get going on a plan that **makes sure that will happen** for you."
Accumulators	Asset Accumulation	"In all our time together we have focused on the simple goal of increasing your assets. We've done a good job of **building up your portfolio.** The next step is to lock in those assets as much as possible with an estate plan focused on continuing to **maximize your wealth."**

(continued) ***High-Net-Worth Personalities***	***Primary Motivation***	***Positioning Retirement & Estate Planning Services***
Gamblers	Thrill of investing	"I know you like options with a little **more risk, and upside potential.** I think we should look at **certain investments** so you can continue to invest as you like, even during retirement."
Innovators	New investment approaches	"I see that you are **substantially above the** marital exemption; we can always use the usual trusts. But you **like innovative and technical solutions so** I suggest we consider a **charitable family limited partnership."**

Think about how you use retirement and estate planning. Is it important in your asset capture or relationship development strategy? How have your clients previously responded to your planning suggestions? Do you have the planning support and resources in place? And, above all, as you think of your top clients as high-net-worth personalities, how might you position your retirement and estate planning services?

Every high-net-worth personality can be motivated to engage in retirement and estate planning for very different reasons. The key to using retirement and estate planning strategies effectively is to understand and leverage those reasons.

The reason a Family Steward would do this sort of planning is to protect the family. This is a forward looking group who worries as

much about grandchildren and even great grandchildren as they do their children. So, how would you explain retirement and estate planning to a Family Steward in a way that will directly appeal to their motivations? You might try something like, "Since taking care of the family is so important to you, I think we should look at estate planning in the light of some new ways we can use to protect your loved ones." Retirement planning often is somewhat less important to Family Stewards. Many stay active in their businesses long after traditional retirement ages and, when they do retire, they maintain their modest life styles.

Financial Phobics might seem to have every reason to avoid retirement and estate planning because of their dislike of investing and their desire to duck financial responsibility. However, they are also fearful, and their fear gives you an opening. How could you explain retirement and estate planning to a Financial Phobic? Remember not to go into technical detail, but to work with their emotion of fear by reassuring them. You might say something like, "I know you get a little frustrated around money, but I think if you know exactly where you are, you will definitely be able to relax. Let me do a retirement analysis for you. I'm almost certain you will see that you will be very well off for the rest of your days, and you should start thinking about what you would like to do with your time."

Personal and financial independence is the goal of Independents.

As a result, they have an especially strong reason to do retirement planning because it is the answer to their dream of golfing around the world. They invest in order to retire, so it is very easy to position retirement planning to this high-net-worth personality. Consider something like, "You want nothing more than to do what you want to do, when you want to do it. I think you are just at the point of being independent, but let's update your retirement plan just to be sure." Estate planning is a little more difficult, as Independents don't envision leaving much behind, but you can link their desire for independence to some of the benefits select trusts can provide.

Getting the Anonymous to open up sufficiently simply to position retirement and estate planning can be a challenge. But as you connect their high-net-worth personality to the retirement and/or estate planning process, and help them see the connection, you get more cooperation from this group. Because the Anonymous are so fearful and worried about personal security and confidentiality, they are not naturally inclined to engage in the kind of disclosure estate planning, in particular, requires.

The Anonymous need constant assurance that you are protecting the integrity of their information during the planning process. How, then, to describe retirement and estate planning to an Anonymous? Try something like, "I know how important the confidentiality of your financial information is to you. To keep things as private as possible, we need to do an estate plan. I have software right here in my PC that will let me do the job, so your data will never leave this office until it's time to talk to a lawyer."

Power is all-important to Moguls. For that reason, Moguls value money because money confers power. Moguls like to control people and things around them. Because of this focus on control, it is quite easy to position retirement and estate planning to a Mogul. Retirement planning is certainly about taking control over your life, and is appealing to Moguls.

"A life at ease is a difficult pursuit."
- William Cowper

Moguls are especially attracted to estate planning because estate planning is a way to exert control over others, even from their graves. In talking about estate planning, be sure to emphasize control issues: "You've told me how you have had to stay on top of your kids because you're not sure how they will handle wealth. If we get on top of that estate planning now, we can set up the kind of good controls you want."

Prestige, recognition, public acknowledgement and status are the motivators for the VIP high-net-worth personality. How could you explain retirement and estate planning to a VIP in terms recognizable and relevant to them? You could position aspects of retirement planning against their affection for material consumption, as in, "You're going to want to have the finer things and the rewards of life when you retire. Let's get going on a plan that makes sure that will happen for you." Estate planning can be positioned the same way, especially when the status and recognition aspects of trusts and private foundations are emphasized, as in, "It's only fitting that you get the recognition you deserve. You might want to consider a private foundation in your name that will continue to let people know of your contributions."

Asset accumulation is the sole objective of Accumulators. Retirement planning interests them less than estate planning, because of its focus on asset conservation. It's a pretty straightforward matter to position estate planning with Accumulators. Because they are so singularly focused on accumulating more assets, you can use that as the primary benefit of estate planning, and say something like, "In all our time together, we have focused on the single goal of increasing your assets. We've done a good job of building up your portfolio. The next step is to lock in those assets as much as possible with an estate plan focused on continuing to maximize your wealth."

Gamblers are extremely well-read and experienced in financial and investment matters. They approach investing with zest, seeking out positions with considerable leverage.

Estate and retirement planning are not intrinsically interesting to this segment, but you can motivate Gamblers by connecting aspects of estate and retirement planning to their personality. You could, for example, say something like, "I know you like options with a little more risk, and upside potential. I think we should look at certain investments so you can continue to invest as you like, even during retirement."

We know about the technical enthusiasm and investment know-how of Innovators. Because they like to be at the forefront of anything new, you need to highlight what is innovating or cutting edge in your planning program.

Innovators are very astute, and you will need to talk over the technical aspects of planning with them as a peer. You may position, say, the trust aspects of estate planning in this way, "I see that you are substantially above the marital exemption; we can always use the usual trusts. But you like innovative and technical solutions so I suggest we consider a charitable family limited partnership."

These examples illustrate the power of delivering a call to action through the principles of high-net-worth psychology. As you can see, this way of describing retirement and estate planning is much more effective and meaningful than non-compelling statements. High-net-worth psychology enables you to connect with the deepest motivations of affluent investors. Put the affluent investor's psychological needs and wants first, and connect everything you are doing with regard to planning to those needs and wants.

Positioning Charitable Planning

More and more affluent investors are turning to charitable planning. Charity appeals to people more as they age, and the wealthiest segment of society is aging quickly. In addition, their professional advisors are showing them how important charitable planning can be in estate planning. Even the government has pitched in and established tax incentives to stimulate charitable giving by affluent individuals.

> ***"Money alone sets the world in motion."***
> ***- Pubilius Syrus***

From an investment advisor's standpoint, charitable planning can be an invaluable tool in asset capture because it gives the advisor a comprehensive overview of a client's portfolio (as we discuss in Chapter 17).

Most affluent people support non-profits with benevolent gifts of cash and their time. Many serve on boards or head committees. However, few have gone to the trouble of forming a comprehensive charitable plan as part of their overall financial planning, and even fewer have conferred a major gift or established a charitable trust or some other planned gift; and fewer still have established private foundations.

Does high-net-worth psychology help you understand the inner values and motivations of the philanthropic affluent? Absolutely. Take, for example, the extent to which people describe themselves as highly philanthropic. Who would you expect would be the least philanthropic—Accumulators? Well, you would be right. Because Accumulators are focused solely on building up their personal assets, we could predict they would be less likely to give away money in large amounts, and the data reveals this.

Taken as a group, affluent clients generally think of themselves as very philanthropic. The most distinctive group are VIPs, all of whom (100%) say they are. Most Family Stewards (91%) described themselves as very philanthropic, as do Innovators (90%), Financial Phobics (89%), Independents (88%), Gamblers (85%), The Anonymous (80%) and Moguls (76%). Less than half (47%) of Accumulators define themselves that way.

Although most high-net-worth personalities think of themselves as highly philanthropic, you still need to position charitable planning services in a unique way to each of the nine types.

Which two or three high-net-worth personalities fit most of your affluent clients? Take a minute to think about how you would position charitable planning to each of them. What will their responses be? How different is the high-net-worth psychology approach from what you do now to promote charitable planning?

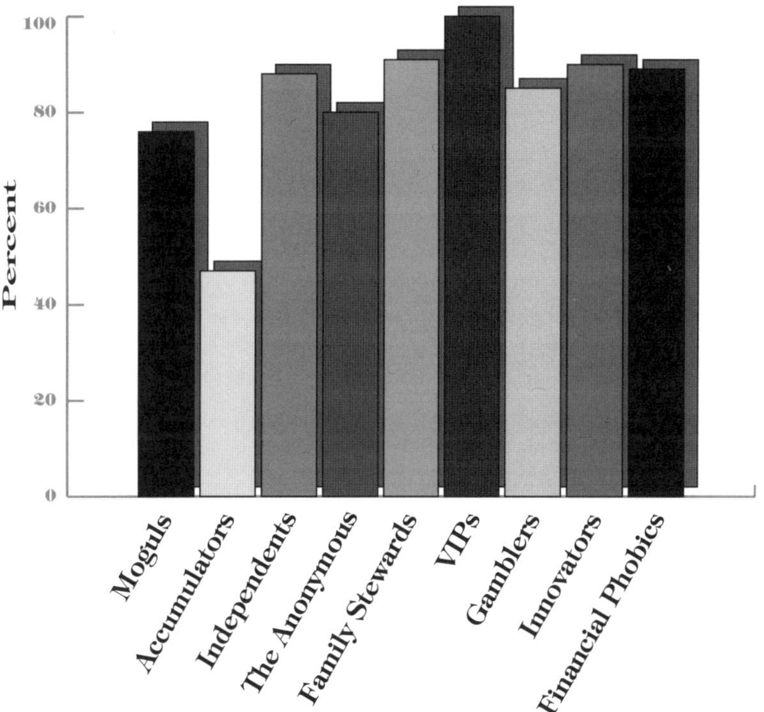

This chapter will help you explain charitable planning to each of your clients based on their high-net-worth psychology. The table below summarizes the various ways to position charitable planning to high-net-worth segments.

Using High-Net-Worth Psychology to Position Charitable Planning

High-Net-Worth Personalities	***Primary Motivation***	***Positioning Charitable Planning***
Family Stewards	Care of the Family	"I know your charities mean a lot to you and I know your **top priority is to take care of your family.** If we do some charitable planning together, I think we can find some ways you can be philanthropic and **still keep your family first."**
Financial Phobics	Avoid financial affairs	"I know how much you are involved with the art museum and the symphony — **have you given any thought to making a major gift?** We could have a look at **your charitable options** if you like."
Independents	Financial Freedom	"I know your goal is to be **financially independent,** and there are ways charitable planning could work well into your plans. There are some things we could look at that will **provide security for you** as well as a gift to charity."
The Anonymous	Confidentiality, privacy	"I admire your charitable activities and I also know how important **confidentiality** is to you. Have you considered ways to make a major gift to charity while still **maintaining your confidentiality?"**

(continued) ***High-Net-Worth Personalities***	***Primary Motivation***	***Positioning Charitable Planning***
Moguls	Power, control	"I know how much you value your **leadership** with the hospital. I wonder if you have considered some charitable planning. I have got some options that could give you **continuing control** over your giving."
VIPs	Status, prestige	"The **best people** have always been philanthropic. You are in a position to consider a private foundation, which would give **your family the prominence it deserves."**
Accumulators	Asset Accumulation	"We know your **top priority is asset accumulation.** However, there are some options you may want to consider in charitable planning. There are some ways we can continue to focus on your goal of **long-term investment performance,** but still support some of the non-profits you have an interest in."
Gamblers	Thrill of investing	"I know you like **the excitement of making a decision** and seeing what happens. There are some charitable options that give you that same involvement. You can continue to **decide** which charities to give to and then **see what happens** as a result."

(continued) *High-Net-Worth Personalities*	*Primary Motivation*	*Positioning Charitable Planning*
Innovators	New investment approaches	"You know that there are **some interesting new twists** to charitable planning. I've looked at a few of these on your behalf and thought you'd be **intrigued by these new developments.**"

Family Stewards tend to have a long history of supporting charity; they are invested in their local communities and want to help build them up. However, they may sense a conflict between giving to charity and financially safeguarding their family. However, there are a number of ways both of these goals can be achieved through proper charitable planning.

So, how would you explain charitable planning to a Family Steward? You might try something like, "I know your charities mean a lot to you, and I know your top priority is to take care of your family. If we do some charitable planning together, I think we can find some ways you can be philanthropic and still keep your family first."

Financial Phobics avoid financial discussions but throw themselves into their friends, family and community. Many are very active in non-profits. For them, it is a very appealing idea to be able to use their financial assets to help their favorite charities. Unfortunately, many of the best ways to accomplish such giving (e.g., charitable trusts) are complex, and can turn off a Financial Phobic. How, then, could you explain these benefits of charitable planning to a Financial Phobic? Again, avoid technical detail, but emphasize the advantages of charitable planning by saying something like, "I know how much you are involved with the art museum and the symphony—have you given any thought to making a major gift? We could have a look at your charitable options if you like."

Because Independents are so focused on financial independence, charitable giving is not at the top of their priority list. However, many are open to it if they can see how charitable giving can figure into a plan for financial security, as it can with certain charitable arrangements. How can you explain charitable planning to an Independent? How about, "I know your goal is to be financially independent, and there are ways charitable planning could work well into your plans. There are some things we could look at that will provide security for you as well as a gift to charity."

The Anonymous are obsessive about their privacy, but often are also very charitably oriented. There are ways they can act on their generous impulses while retaining their privacy. You can be successful positioning charitable planning to the Anonymous. You could approach an Anonymous client with something like, "I admire your charitable activities and I also know how important confidentiality is to you. Have you considered ways to make a major gift to charity while still maintaining your confidentiality?"

Moguls act out their power needs through all the institutions with which they are involved, and non-profits are no exception. Moguls tend to serve in leadership positions on non-profit boards, and also are generous givers because it affords them a certain amount of leverage and power. You can effectively position charitable planning to a Mogul by emphasizing control: "I know how much you value your leadership with the hospital. I wonder if you have considered some charitable planning. I have got some options that could give you continuing control over your giving."

Of all the high-net-worth personalities, VIPs are the most involved in non-profits because participation in many non-profits is itself a symbol of prestige and status. VIPs like to be surrounded with social leaders, and non-profits serve as a place these people congregate.

> ***"The best portion of***
> ***a good man's life,***
> ***His little, nameless,***
> ***unremembered acts***
> ***Of kindness and love."***
> ***- William Wordsworth***

Positioning charitable planning to a VIP is straightforward, simply position it as the preferred investment approach of social leaders, "The best people have always been philanthropic. You are in a position to consider a private foundation, which would give your family the prominence it deserves."

The high-net-worth personality least likely to be open to charitable giving (and to charitable planning) is Accumulators. Accumulators are focused on just one goal—accumulating more assets.

Because of this focus, they are not particularly interested in giving their hard-won assets away. However, some may be interested if charitable planning is properly positioned: "We know your top priority is asset accumulation. However, there are some options you may want to consider in charitable planning. There are some ways we can continue to focus on your goal of long-term investment performance, but still support some of the non-profits you have an interest in."

Long-term charitable planning is deemed too far off for Gamblers, who often prefer active involvement in short-term investing. Gamblers love the excitement of investing. Test to see if a Gambler could be interested in the excitement of giving and doing good—many are. You could position some charitable vehicles in this way, "I know you like the excitement of making a decision and seeing what happens. There are some charitable options that give you that same involvement. You can continue to decide which charities to give to and then see what happens as a result."

Innovators are attracted to interesting and new ways of managing money; the tax advantages of charitable alternatives have this appeal for Innovators. When you approach them about charitable planning, you should emphasize the technical, innovative or unusual aspects of the approaches you are bringing forward. Bring supporting materials and be prepared to dive into the details: "You know that there are some interesting new twists to charitable planning. I've looked at a few of these on your behalf and thought you'd be intrigued by these new developments."

Who are the philanthropic affluent? They are charitably inclined wealthy individuals, and most wealthy people are considerably generous. Major giving today is very technical, and the philanthropic affluent need the services of top-flight financial advisors. The key to working effectively with the philanthropic affluent is charitable planning. By doing charitable planning, you are leveraging the advantages of charitable planning for your current clients, and you will become known to a new set of clients.

Currently, one of the most potent market opportunities is charitable planning as an entry into asset capture. Most wealthy people are charitably inclined and need experts in the charitable estate process to help them. That most investment advisors do not possess this expertise creates new opportunities for you. Opportunities for asset capture emerge naturally through the charitable planning process.

IV

Keeping Affluent Investors

16

High-Impact Relationship Management: The I-CLAS Model

When clients judge you, research shows they use five factors to gauge their satisfaction with you. These five factors are:

> *"Cheshire puss," Alice began, "...Would you please tell me which way I ought to go from here?" "That depends on where you want to get to," said the cat.*
>
> *- Lewis Carroll*

- Investment performance
- Client orientation
- Leadership
- Attending behaviors
- Shared values

We refer to these five components as "I-CLAS." The hyphen indicates a distinction between investment performance and the four factors leading to satisfaction with the relationship.

It should come as no surprise that clients judge you according to investment performance and service. However, what is surprising is the level of importance placed on these two areas. Research shows that clients regard the relationship as four times more important than investment performance in overall satisfaction.

The I-CLAS Model

I	Investment Performance	**C**	**Client Orientation**
		L	**Leadership**
		A	**Attending Behaviors**
		S	**Shared Values**

Again, affluent clients regard CLAS (Relationship Factors) as four times more important than I (Investment Performance).

Clearly, investment performance alone will not carry the day. Investment performance accounts for only a relatively small portion of your clients' overall evaluation of you.

The good news is that investment advisors who can deliver solid investment performance combined with high-quality customer service are well positioned to increase the amount of assets on deposit per affluent client, as well as win referrals from their current clients.

The research on this is compelling, as you will see.

Another way of looking at the importance of these factors in the client's mind is to examine why clients leave their investment advisors. Of all affluent clients who fired their investment advisors, just 13% did so because of investment performance. Most (87%) left because they were unhappy with the relationship (the CLAS) factors.

Why Clients Leave

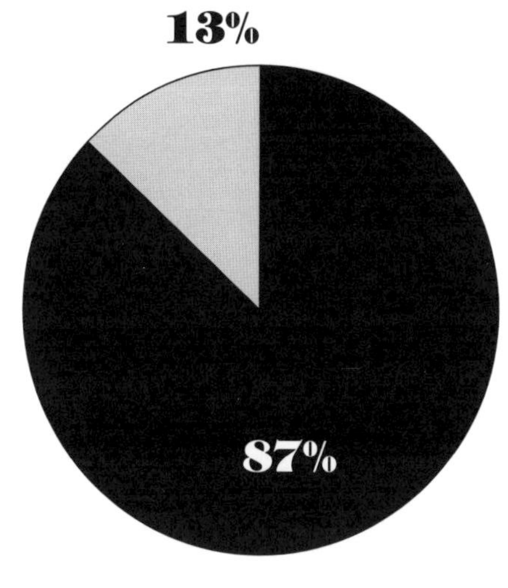

Are you ready for a surprise? Clients will leave even if investment performance is high. In fact, 96% of the clients who fired their advisors because of the relationship were "very happy" with investment performance.

As you can see, if your relationship with your clients is strong, your business will be strong as well. One in four highly satisfied clients increases assets under management each year. Better still, nine out of 10 highly satisfied affluent clients will refer at least one person who becomes a client. The operative words here are "becomes a client," not just a referral.

Good Relationships Lead to Referrals

Nine out of 10 highly satisfied clients will refer at least one person who becomes a client.

It is clear that relationship factors are critically important to the satisfaction of your clients and the ultimate success of your investment advisory business.

Now we should focus on how you should build up your relationship factors. How can you be sure you are doing the right thing to build better relationships with your clients? How can you be sure you are doing your best with respect to high-impact relationship management?

CLAS:

Key Elements of Each Area for A Practical Understanding

 ***lient Orientation***

1. Time Management—the way you use your time in working with your clients
2. Addressing client needs thouroughly
3. Fostering client involvement and participation

 ***eadership***

1. Technical prowess
2. Emphasis on quality
3. Passion for service

 ***ttending Behaviors***

1. Client originated contacts
2. Advisor originated contacts
3. Total number of contacts

 ***hared Values***

1. Similar belief system
2. Appropriate manners
3. Trustworthiness

Key Elements of Each Area for a Practical Understanding

The "C" of CLAS is Client Orientation. There are a few things on which to concentrate when it comes to Client Orientation. The first is time management, which is the way you use your time in working with your clients. The second is addressing client needs thoroughly. The third is fostering client involvement and participation in the planning and investment process.

The "L" of CLAS is Leadership. Leadership is comprised of several components, the first of which is your technical prowess. Leadership also includes an emphasis on quality and a passion for service.

The "A" of CLAS is Attending Behaviors, signifying the actual contacts between you and your clients. When you think of attending behaviors you should be sensitive to the number of and reason for contacts originated by your clients. Conversely, you also should be aware of the number of and reason for client contacts that you originate. Finally, notice the total number of contacts.

The "S" of CLAS is Shared Values. You should concentrate on this trio of aspects of shared values. The first is similar belief systems; the second is appropriate manners; and, the third is trustworthiness.

The question now remains how can you implement this model? How can you put Client Orientation, Leadership, Attending Behaviors and Shared Values into practice? The answer is high-net-worth psychology.

High-net-worth psychology provides you with key insights into a client's motivations and goals. By understanding these motivations and goals better, you can easily identify meaningful relationship and service aspects on which you can improve, and deliver them more consistently.

Let's take one example to illustrate how to implement the CLAS model. One of your top clients is a Family Steward who, like other Family Stewards, is motivated to invest by the goal of securing their family's future. If you are to apply the "C" (Client Orientation) of "CLAS" to a Family Steward, you need to think about the aspects of client orientation. How should you use your time in working with this Family Steward? How should you address a Family Steward's needs thoroughly? How should you foster a Family Steward's involvement and participation? Here are a few suggestions. Follow your client's lead in involving other key family members in the process, and invest time in this effort. You should also be mindful of remembering family occasions such as birthdays and anniversaries. Make sure your meeting times do not conflict with family activities, such as a daughter's soccer game. Naturally, what you do with a Family Steward client will depend on both you and your client, but this system gives you a basic checklist to follow.

> ***"There are no such things as service industries. There are only industries whose service components are greater or less than those of other industries. Everybody is in service."***
> ***- Theodore Levitt***

Let's take the example one step further. How should you apply the "L" of Leadership to this Family Steward? Think about how you show your client your technical prowess, quality and a passion for service.

Some suggestions for showing leadership to a Family Steward include emphasizing your experience in working with family issues, and stress reassurance when you talk about performance. Again, you will tailor exactly how you communicate leadership based on your individual client, but this provides you with a framework.

Moving on to the "A" of "Attending Behaviors," you should be sensitive to the number of and reason for contacts originated by your clients, the number of and reason for client contacts that you originate and the total number of contacts. Family Stewards generally require a lot of reassurance so you should schedule customary face-to-face meetings. Also, be sure these meetings follow a regular, predictable pattern. If a Family Steward starts calling you frequently, you are not giving them enough attention.

The "S" of "Shared Values" suggests that you concentrate on shared values, similar belief systems, appropriate manners and trustworthiness. How could you communicate these to a Family Steward client? Try something like talking about the importance of family in your own life. You also could give examples of how your personal value of thrift benefits your family. Again, you will customize these suggestions to your own situation and client.

The following matrix will give you ideas for how to apply these four principles.

"Look at our balance sheet. On the asset side, you can see so-and-so many aircrafts worth so-and-so many billions. But it is wrong; we are fooling ourselves. What we should put on the balance sheet is last year SAS carried so-and-so many happy passengers. Because that is the only asset we've got — people who are happy with our service and willing to come back and pay for it again."

- Jan Carlson

	Client Orientation	Leadership
Family Steward	• *Involves key family members*	• *Emphasize experience in working with family issues*
	• *Remember family occasions*	• *When talking about performance, stress reassurance*
Financial Phobics	• *Avoid technical discussions*	• *Encourage client trust by talking about perfectionism*
	• *Learn a lot about their outside interests*	• *Frequently inform them of high quality performance, but do not spend a lot of time on it*
Independents	• *Be task driven, and focused on the client goal*	• *Always talk about investment performance in the context of the client's goal—financial freedom*
	• *Avoid technical discussions irrelevant to the client's goal*	• *Talk about successful experiences in working with similar clients*
the Anonymous	• *Great attention to client privacy needs*	• *Explore client preferences for maintaining privacy*
	• *Talk about firm commitment to client confiden-tiality*	• *Tell client about the firm's security procedures*
Moguls	• *Reinforce perception of client control at all opportunities*	• *Make them feel as though they are the #1 client*

	Client Orientation	Leadership
Moguls (cont'd)	• *Create decision-points for client (opportunities to make decisions among several options)*	• *Make them feel as through they are working with the #1 firm in terms of investment performance and service*
VIPs	• *Provide "first class" treatment (board room, best restaurants)*	• *Make them feel as though they are in the same class as celebrity clients*
	• *Give the sense of many people involved on their behalf*	• *Stress sterling image of the firm*
Accumulators	• *Communicate a sense of urgency around financial performance*	• *Report frequently on superior performance compared to selected benchmarks*
	• *Involve their other professional advisors (lawyers, CPA, etc.)*	• *In every interaction, reinforce investment expertise*
Gamblers	• *Communicate excitement and enthusiasm for investing*	• *Emphasize expertise in taking advantage of market movements and volatility*
	• *Highest possible interaction with portfolio manager*	• *Communicate trading vs. buy-and-hold orientation*
Innovators	• *Want access to top technical expertise*	• *Bring leading edge investment opportunities*
	• *Position yourself as an educational resource*	• *Talk the technical jargon*

	Attending Behaviors	Shared Values
Family Steward	• *Schedule regular face-to-face meetings*	• *Share the importance of your own family in your life*
	• *Arrange meetings so that they follow a regular predict-able pattern*	• *Show how your value of thrift benefits the family*
Financial Phobics	• *Fewer meetings*	• *Show interest in their lives*
	• *Meetings focus on life style (not financial) issues*	• *Talk about your belief that investing is necessary, but that not everyone has to be an expert*
Independents	• *Frequent updates on progress toward the goal of financial independence*	• *Tell stories about how other clients who have lived out their dreams*
	• *Periodic review of the financial objective*	• *Talk about how appealing you think the idea of financial freedom is*
the Anonymous	• *Fewer meetings than most clients*	• *Agree that privacy is increasingly important*
	• *Short agenda because of time constraints*	• *Say you like working with clients who understand the need for confidentiality*
Moguls	• *Meetings organized around decisions they are asked to make*	• *Show that you think their accomplishments are significant*

	Attending Behaviors	Shared Values
Moguls (cont'd)	• *Reinforce previous client decisions*	• *Set up choices for the client, don't question their decisions*
VIPs	• *Schedule frequent meetings to address their ego needs*	• *Drop off names of celebrity clients of the firm*
	• *Ensure that meeting content is not exceedingly challenging*	• *Talk about highly visible people in the community*
Accumulators	• *Conduct frequent meetings*	• *Reinforce the value of accumulating wealth*
	• *Focus all meetings on portfolio results*	• *Show belief that "private wealth is what made this country great"*
Gamblers	• *Initiate many phone contacts between meetings*	• *Mirror their emotional intensity*
	• *Quickly respond to clients*	• *Show you share an appreciation for quickness, risk-taking, and action*
Innovators	• *Have frequent interactions (not just meetings)*	• *Share belief that innovative, cutting edge investing is the way to go*
	• *Focus on industry news, and new products*	• *Reflect their technical turn of mind*

High-impact relationship management is the key to client retention. The I-CLAS model forces you to focus on the factors that keep clients with you — client orientation, leadership, attending behaviors and shared values along with investment performance. If you create high levels of satisfaction among your clients by focusing on these principles, you can expect asset capture and client referrals and introductions.

The Asset Capture Process

> *"Money is power, freedom, a cushion, the root of all evil, the sum of all blessings."*
> ***- Carl Sandberg***

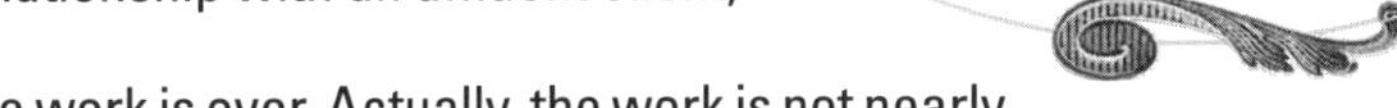

It is vital to sustain your wealthy investor relation-ships and leverage them. You may feel that after you have put in a lot of effort to create a relationship with an affluent client, the work is over. Actually, the work is not nearly over. You must to continue to invest time and effort in that relationship.

The reason is asset capture. The average wealthy client has three investment advisory relationships. In almost all cases, you are managing only a piece of their portfolios. If you are the most recent advisor, you are managing just a small piece. This is why you need to continue to put effort into the relationship. In fact, there are three major reasons to invest in every affluent client relationship.

Major Reason #1: The more you invest in the relationship, the more likely you are to have a very satisfied wealthy client.

Major Reason #2: The more satisfied the wealthy client, the more likely they are to entrust you with more of their assets. Good

relationship management results in more asset capture.

Major Reason #3: The more satisfied the wealthy client, the more likely they are to refer their peers to you. Good relationship management results in new affluent clients (see Chapter 7).

Again, the fact is that affluent investors (especially those with more than $1 million in investable assets) have an average of three to four investment advisors. The larger the portfolio, the more likely an investor is to have multiple investment advisors.

To put this in perspective, think about your own clients and answer these questions:

1. For your average clients, what percentage of their portfolios are you managing?
2. For your top 10 clients, what percentage of their portfolios are you managing?

If you are like most investment advisors, you will have one of two answers to both of these questions. Answer #1 usually is, "I don't know." Answer #2 usually is, "There is a lot I am not managing."

Multiple Investment Advisors and High-Net-Worth Psychology

In the following table, an investor's high-net-worth personality drives the decision to use multiple investment advisors. At one end of the spectrum are Accumulators and Innovators, who use many investment advisors because they want to tap into the greatest amount of expertise possible.

Probability of Having Multiple Investment Advisors by High-Net-Worth Personality

High-Net-Worth Personality	Core Investment Motivation	Probability of Using Multiple Advisors
Accumulators	Wealth	High
Innovators	Cutting edge products	High
Moguls	Power	Medium-High
VIPs	Status and prestige	Medium-High
Gamblers	Excitement	Medium-High
Family Stewards	Safeguard the Family	Medium
Independents	Financial independence	Medium
The Anonymous	Confidentiality	Low
Financial Phobics	Dislike investing	Low

Accumulators use various investment advisors because they want to get the best support for their goal of wealth accumulation. Innovators do so because they want access to all the latest investment innovations. If you have an Accumulator or an Innovator as a client, you stand a good chance of asset capture if you meet their specific needs. However, do not expect to end up with their entire portfolio, because both these types believe that no one investment advisor will have all the answers they seek.

At the other end of the spectrum are the Anonymous and the Financial Phobics, both of whom are unlikely to use more than one investment manager. The Anonymous will concentrate all, or nearly all, their assets with one investment advisor because they are reluctant to disclose their financial situation. Financial Phobics will concentrate their business with a single investment advisor because they want the simplicity of dealing with one manager.

These two high-net-worth personalities can be excellent new prospects if you find they have become unhappy with their current investment advisors. In the case of the Anonymous, their discontent will arise because they no longer feel their affairs are being handled with the right degree of confidentiality. In the case of Financial Phobics, dissatisfaction will stem from something having soured in their personal relationship with their current investment advisor.

The other five high-net-worth personalities fall in between these two extremes, and they make excellent targets for an asset capture strategy. The trend of using multiple investment advisors can work to your benefit. Most affluent investors know they need to bring "new blood" into their investment systems from time to time, and they often try out a new advisor with a small portion of their portfolio.

None of the Family Stewards, Independents, Moguls, VIPs, Accumulators, Gamblers or Innovators in our research have one advisor for all their investment needs. All have multiple investment advisors, some as many as five.

One-Stop Shopping

We asked affluent clients, "Suppose the investment advisor you have the strongest relationship with came to you and said, 'Because

How Many Investment Advisors?

High-Net-Worth Personality	One Advisor	Two or More Advisors
The Anonymous	79%	21%
Financial Phobics	63%	37%
Family Stewards	0%	100%
Moguls	0%	100%
Accumulators	0%	100%
Innovators	0%	100%
Independents	0%	100%
VIPs	0%	100%
Gamblers	0%	100%

of the recent merger between my firm and the other company, I can now provide you with all the financial services you need—from life insurance to money management and banking and trust services.' How likely would you be to let your closest advisor manage all your financial affairs?"

Basically, the one-stop-shopping concept is appealing to the same two high-net-worth personalities already predisposed to the concept — Financial Phobics and the Anonymous. The few Financial Phobics and Anonymous who do not already use just one financial advisor all say they would like to. Among the other high-net-worth personalities (none of whom had already consolidated their financial affairs), just 18% of Accumulators, 5% of Moguls, 3% of Independents and 2% of Family Stewards said they would consolidate under their closest advisor given a merger situation, as mentioned above.

Will You Consolidate Assets?

High-Net-Worth Personality	% Saying Yes if Their Current Best Advisor Asked Them to Consolidate
Financial Phobics	37%
The Anonymous	21%
Accumulators	18%
Moguls	5%
Independents	3%
Family Stewards	2%
Innovators	0%
VIPs	0%
Gamblers	0%

Taken together, just 22% of affluent investors respond quite favorably to the idea of single financial advisor relationships. The other 78% want to have relationships with several different financial advisors.

Why Not Single Investment Advisor Relationships?

Why is it that most affluent investors do not like the idea of single investment advisor relationships? There are several reasons. In fact, each high-net-worth personality has a different reason for not liking single investment advisor relationships (except for Financial Phobics and the Anonymous, who like the idea).

For example, Family Stewards are loyal often to a fault. Their loyalty to their families drives their investment activity. As business owners, they value multiple supplier relationships. They also know the best way to protect their families interests is to have multiple investment advisory relationships.

The more sophisticated personalities like Innovators, Gamblers and Accumulators feel that single investment advisor relationships would deprive them of the hot information or technical expertise that multiple investment advisors could bring to their situations. VIPs don't want to consolidate into one advisory relationship because they want to preserve their access to multiple prestigious investment advisory firms. Moguls also do not want to consolidate because that would

Why Not Single Investment Advisor Relationships?

Reason for Disliking Single Advisor Relationships Idea	% Giving Reason	Key Segments
I feel more secure with several advisors	33%	Family Stewards, Independents
Each one is expert in something different	26%	Innovators, Accumulators
Financial services are too complicated for one person to do it all	22%	Innovators, Gamblers
I have a history with each advisor and am loyal to each	16%	Family Stewards
I can play my advisors off one another	16%	Moguls

change the power dynamics in the client-advisor relationship; with multiple investment advisors, Moguls can, and commonly do, play investment advisors off one another. Independents, who seek freedom, are commonly price sensitive, and prefer having multiple investment advisors because they can compare fees. In short, there are as many reasons to respond negatively to single advisor relationships as there are high-net-worth personalities.

As you can see, single investment advisor relationships are not the norm for the affluent. Except for two of the high-net-worth personalities, most are not inclined to work with just one single investment advisor.

However, their desire to steer clear of single relationships does not mean they are unwilling to obtain a number of different financial services from one high-quality financial advisor. There are two positives on which you may focus. The first is that increasingly, advisors can provide a broad range of financial services and products, and investors will pick and choose both products and advisors. The success of high-end insurance producers is proof of this. Insurance providers have had great success in recent years expanding the range of services they provide—especially as they have moved into the investment advisory business.

Second, and more importantly, wealthy people make their buying decisions on the basis of their personal relationships with their advisors, not on the basis of the institution providing those products.

In summary, the wealthy want to keep their options open and maintain several investment advisor relationships. By and large, they are not interested in a single investment advisor relationship. However, the potential benefit for you is that it is highly possible for a talented and knowledgeable investment advisor to be effectively positioned to oversee the majority of a wealthy investor's portfolio.

Increasing Assets Under Management Per Client

Is it easier to get more assets from a current wealthy client or to find a new wealthy client? Obviously, the answer is that it is much easier to garner more assets from current clients. In studying the best practices of elite investment advisors, we have been able to document the asset capture process. This is the process many of the more successful investment advisors are using to gain a bigger share of their affluent clients' wallets.

There are three steps in the asset capture process:

- Step I: Build High-Impact Relationship Management
- Step II: Identify Asset Transfer Opportunities
- Step III: Ask for the Additional Assets

Step I: Build High-Impact Relationship Management

Remember the discussion about client satisfaction and client referrals? Remember that client satisfaction was the key to personal introductions and client referrals? Well, client satisfaction also is the key to asset capture.

In the private wealth industry, you build a highly successful investment advisory business one happy and satisfied affluent client

at a time. Two things make for happy clients: investment performance and the quality of the relationship. The problem is that you can't control investment performance. That is, you can't guarantee above average investment performance every quarter. Unfortunately, you can't always rely on investment performance for happy and satisfied clients.

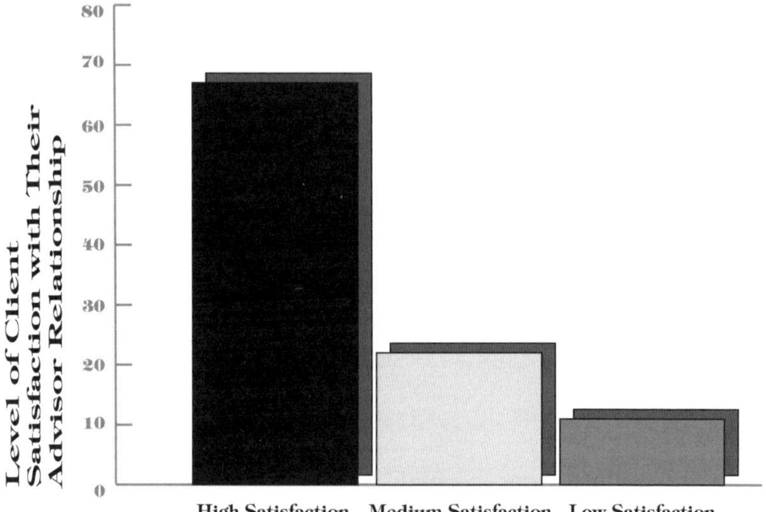

On the other hand, you do have just about complete control over the quality of your interpersonal relationships with your clients. You have it within your power to generate very satisfied clients through the high-quality interpersonal relationships you build, and very satisfied clients will give you more and more of their assets to manage.

High-impact relationship management results in clients adding assets. The greater the satisfaction clients derive from their interpersonal relationship with you, the more likely they are to add assets.

Exceptional investment performance is the only reason affluent clients who are dissatisfied with their interpersonal relationship with their investment advisors will add assets. As you might expect, when investment performance is no longer exceptional, these affluent clients quickly move on to another advisor.

Let's take a moment for you to assess the quality of your relationship with some of your affluent clients using a scale like this one:

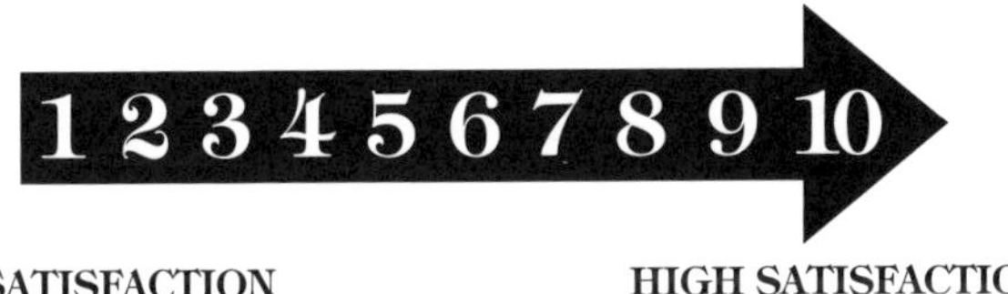

List 10 of your affluent clients on a sheet of paper. Next to each name, write a number from this scale to show how satisfied you think they are with their personal relationship with you.

Which ones did you rate an 8, 9 or 10? These are your top asset capture opportunities. They are already very satisfied with their relationship with you. These are the clients you should focus on in Step II of the asset capture process.

Beware, though. The clients you rated 1—7 are asset capture targets for other investment advisors. You should take immediate steps to upgrade the quality of your interpersonal relationships with these clients (as we discussed in the previous chapter). In other words, your top priority should be improving your relationship with these clients. Until they are more satisfied with their personal relationship with you, they are not good targets for asset capture strategies.

Step II: Identify Asset Transfer Opportunities

The next step is to get a picture of the overall asset position of your clients — what they have and who is managing it. To do so, you will usually have to perform some sort of planning process for these clients. Any one of the following planning approaches will put you in the position of figuring out what assets you are not managing, and they all set the stage for Step III of the asset capture processes. The planning approaches include:

- Estate planning;
- Retirement planning;
- Asset allocation planning;
- Asset protection planning; and
- Charitable giving planning.

The reason we select these approaches is that for each one you will need to do a comprehensive analysis of the client's entire portfolio. By providing one or more of these planning services, you will be able to identify pools of assets that other investment advisors are managing, and, once identified, target these asset pools for capture.

Such a planning process will also let you find out why other investment advisors are being used, information essential for you to position yourself. A comprehensive planning process also will enable to you figure out situational triggers that will set the stage for your Stage III asset capture.

Situational Triggers

Situational Triggers	Examples
Tax Laws	New capitas gain rules; changes in estate taxes
Family Changes	Divorce; remarriage; birth of a grandchild; impending retirement
Market Changes	Rebalancing; strategic actions
Portfolio	Retirement (rollovers); inheritance

A situational trigger is any meaningful change in the tax laws, in a wealthy client's portfolio, their life or the market. These are excellent times to approach affluent clients and ask for more assets. For example, when the market took a temporary nosedive in October 1997, some astute and quick-acting investment advisors brought in substantial new assets per client by focusing on high-impact relationship management (as you will see in the case study later in this chapter).

Step III: Ask for Additional Assets

Occasionally, as with personal introductions and client referrals, high-impact relationship management alone will prompt affluent clients to bring new assets without your having to directly ask. Once in a while, exceptional investment performance will result in a wealthy client coming to you with more assets. However, by and large, you will have to be proactive, and direct your asset capture strategy. In short, you will have to ask for the additional assets.

Many investment advisors say that asking for more money is difficult. Here are some things to keep in mind to make it easier. First of all, the only clients you are asking are ones that are happy and satisfied (remember, you rated them all an 8, 9 or 10 in their satisfaction with you). Second, you know exactly what assets you are going after because you have completed a comprehensive review of their portfolios while you were assisting them with one of the planning processes we suggested in Step II. Third, and finally, you have picked your moment and are alert for exactly the right time to make the suggestion; that is, you have waited for the change of circumstance—the situational trigger.

There are some ways you can better attune yourself to your clients, potentially garnering additional assets.

The Four-Point Method of Asking for Additional Assets. The best investment advisors we know all work with some form of a four-point approach, although they have customized it to their own ways of doing business with clients. The key points are:

1. **Set Expectations.** Your clients should be reminded from time to time that you are interested in their overall well-being

and that this might include taking into account the way other investment advisors are managing their monies.

2. **Client Review of the Relationship.** Periodically find out from your clients what they like and don't like about your relationship with them.

3. **Ask for More Assets.** You still have to ask. High-net-worth psychology will insure that you position your suggestion most effectively.

4. **Thank the Client.** Let them know you appreciate the trust they have in you.

The Asset Capture Process Works

The asset capture process works, and it works quite well. We have the data to prove it. We networked until we found 41 investment advisors interested in asset capture but who had not received **ANY** additional assets from their wealthy investor clients in the past two years. We trained these investment advisors in high-impact relationship management and provided periodic coaching. We also tracked their asset capture rates.

Every investment advisor in the group added new assets from existing clients during the year following their training. The increase in total assets under management ranged from a solid 15% to a whopping 256%.

Let's put this in perspective. Say you have 10 highly satisfied clients you decide you would like to target for asset capture. Suppose each of these clients currently has $100,000 with you. If your success

matches the success of our advisors, then you, at a minimum, will be managing an additional $150,000 plus in assets. At best you could be managing an extra $2.56 million. And, that's based on just 10 clients. Now, suppose each of these clients currently has $1 million with you. If your success matches that of our group, then you, at a minimum, will be managing an additional $1.5 million more. At best, you could be managing another $25.6 million. It bears repeating that this is based on just 10 clients.

High-impact relationship management results in successful asset capture. Throw in high-net-worth psychology and you have two powerful tools you can use in your own asset capture process.

Case Study: The October '97 Correction

On October 24, 1997, the stock market began to decline and continued throughout next day. On Oct. 27, the DJIA had its largest one-day point decline ever. This market meltdown presented a tremendous opportunity for some investment advisors. In fact, the final week in October proved to be one of the best business development periods for investment advisors who were ready and motivated to take advantage of the opportunity.

To examine the asset capture process in action, we conducted a survey of investment advisors from three different categories—stockbrokers, financial planners/independent investment advisors and private bankers/trust officers.

Our first question was "Did they engage in high-impact relationship management during this time? Specifically, did they initiate contact with their affluent clients during the dark days of Oct. 24 - 27?"

The answer was no. Just 18% of investment advisors initiated contact with their clients during this period; 82% did not. Slightly more than 20% of brokers and financial planners/independent investment advisors proactively approached selected clients. Only 8% of private bankers/trust officers did so.

Few Investment Advisors Contacted Their Clients During the 1997 Market Crisis

Investment Advisor	% Who Contacted	% Who Did Not Contact	Sample Size
Brokers	21%	79%	243
Financial Planners/ Independent Investment Advisors	22%	78%	189
Private Bankers/ Trust Officers	8%	92%	137
All Investment Advisors	18%	82%	569

The next consideration was how many clients did these advisors call? Investment advisors initiated contact with about 14 clients each. The brokers performed best with 17 clients but were closely followed by the financial planners/independent investment advisors who each had 12 clients, and private bankers/trust officers who did call reached an average of eight clients.

Average Number of Clients Contacted

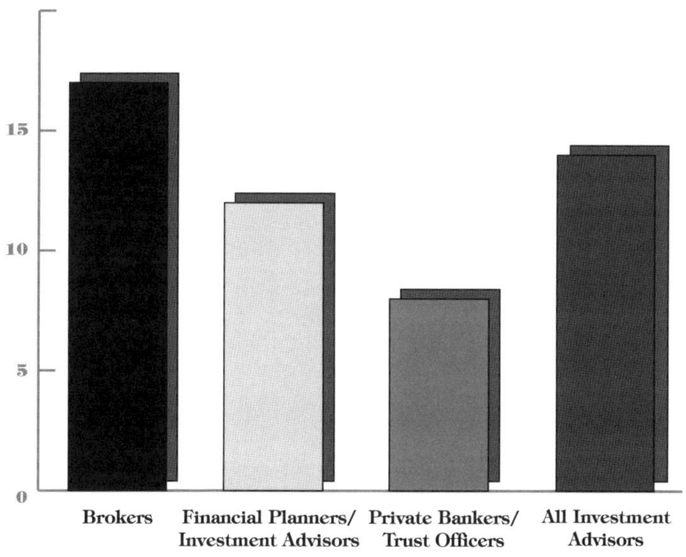

Incremental Assets

Here is evidence that high-impact relationship management works in an asset capture process. Contacting clients during times of crisis (high-impact relationship management) results in asset capture (32% of the clients reached moved assets to the advisors' account).

Client Contacted Providing Additional Assets

Investment Advisor	Total # of Clients Contacted	% Providing Additional Assets
Brokers	867	26%
Financial Planners/ Independent Investment Advisors	504	42%
Private Bankers/ Trust Officers	77	31%
All Investment Advisors	1,448	32%

There are very good reasons for an investment advisor to proactively contact his or her clients in times of crisis. One reason is that stronger relationships result. Another is opportunity for asset capture. For the market crisis example, one in three clients contacted decided to redirect more assets to the advisor to manage. These monies were transferred to the investment advisor before the markets opened on Oct. 28.

Of the 1,448 clients contacted by 104 investors; 32% of them entrusted more assets to the investment advisor to manage. Financial planners/independent investment advisors proved most successful (42%). Private bankers/trust officers and brokers received additional assets from about one-third of the clients they contacted (31% and 26% respectively).

The average amount of additional assets to be managed per client contacted was $260,000. Combined, the 104 investment advisors who contacted their clients during the marker upheaval brought in nearly $120 million in additional assets to be managed.

The private bankers/trust officers obtained the most assets per client (on average, $315,000). They were followed by the financial

planners/investment advisors, who obtained approximately $280,000 per client. The brokers captured, on average, $235,000 per client.

Why Investment Advisors Did Not Contact Their Clients

If carrying out high-impact relationship management during times of crisis is good for business, why did so few investment advisors function this way? We asked the 465 investment advisors who did not contact their best clients during this time why they chose not to do so.

To some extent, many of these reasons are justified. When markets are in crisis, investment advisors are very busy. A lot of issues will consume valuable time that could otherwise be used to contact clients. However, these numbers prove that putting clients first, as high-impact relationship management instructs us, makes an enormous difference. When you do not administer high-impact relationship management, the results are equally predictable. Not one of the investment advisors who did not call clients because of all the aforementioned reasons obtained new assets from their clients.

Reasons for Not Contacting Clients

Reason	Brokers	Financial Planners/ Investment Advisors	Private Bankers/ Trust Officers	All Investment Advisors
Busy putting out fires	84%	74%	66%	76%
Busy handling incoming calls	78%	55%	61%	66%
Busy evaluating the market	51%	67%	72%	62%
Too early to contact clients	46%	35%	58%	46%
Fear of clients being upset	33%	33%	44%	36%

Using High-Net-Worth Psychology

To make high-impact relationship management really work for investment advisors means being prepared and focused when the

client is contacted. To be most successful, investment advisors use high-net-worth psychology when they initiate contact.

Let's presume that an investment advisor contacted his or her clients during the crisis. The following sets of statements are examples of how an investment advisor can customize the way he or she reassures a client:

- Family Stewards: "As we've discussed, markets go up and down. What's happening in the market is not going to hurt us in the long-term. You're still going to have the monies to take care of your family the way we talked about."

- Financial Phobics: "Something's going on in the stock market. I'm carefully watching it for you. By the way, how are the kids?"

- Independents: "This is the market volatility we've been expecting. The fundamentals still look really good. Let's keep our eye on things and stay focused on your goal of early retirement. Over the next few months we want to make sure we're on target for your early retirement."

- The Anonymous: "Remember the private memos I sent you about market volatility? This is what we expected. I want to assure you that I'm watching things carefully. I've put together a confidential analysis just for you. You'll have the confidential analysis later today and we'll talk about what steps we should take."

- Accumulators: "Let's understand both things going on. Concerning your principal, this is a bump in the road we've been expecting. Market fundamentals are still very good so I'm confident we'll achieve our aggressive growth objectives. Of course, the other thing going on is our opportunity to accumulate stocks that will appreciate."

- Moguls: "Our inside view is that this is the correction we've been waiting for. We want to take the high ground, so you have to decide when you want to make your move."

- VIPs: "We've pulled together some of our top people to review the situation for our most important clients, like you. We see that our more astute investors are taking advantage of the situation."
- Gamblers: "This is certainly a thrilling time. It's time to think about what plays we should be making here to take advantage of what's going on in the market."
- Innovators: "This is all very exciting. Let's look at what opportunities exist. All the volatility in the market calls for some state-of-the-art investment thinking."

Of course, the exact wording of the reassurance call as well as how the conversation progresses is a function of the particular affluent client and the investment advisor. Nevertheless, the advantage of using high-net-worth psychology is to ensure the focus is on the needs and wants of affluent investors.

Remember, you are probably not your wealthy client's only investment advisor.

Some high-net-worth personalities could want you to be their only investment advisor, while others will want one or two or three other investment advisors in addition to you.

Does this make asset capture impossible? Not at all. The pools of assets moving among investment advisors to the wealthy are fluid. High-impact relationship management will yield consistent success in asset capture.

There are a number of times when circumstances — trigger events — set the stage for investment advisors to create stronger relationships with their affluent clients. The massive crisis in the stock market that we saw from Oct. 24 — 27, 1997 is one such event. You should be on the lookout for others.

A number of investment advisors saw the situation for what it was — a tremendous opportunity to build more bridges to wealthy clients and a chance to capture additional assets. However, what was telling was that the greater majority of investment advisors did not see the market meltdown in this way.

Regardless of what happens in the stock markets, those investment advisors who focus on the needs and wants of their wealthy clients,

who understand what's important to their wealthy clients as evidenced by using high-net-worth psychology and who actively take advantage of key opportunities to enhance their relationships with their clients will be the most successful investment advisors.

268

V
Taking Action

Creating Client-Focused Marketing Plans

Marketing is the critical success factor in markets where products are commodities. In the financial services industry, products certainly have become commodities. For all the talk of institutional branding, on the one hand, and portfolio manager-as-celebrity, on the other, financial products are still commodities from the perspective of the high-net-worth investor.

> ***"Wine maketh merry: but money answers all things."***
>
> ***- Ecclesiastes, 10:19***

How should an investment advisor respond? The short answer is marketing. In order to thrive, investment advisors need to focus on marketing rather than technical skills, the premise of this book.

Marketing is the set of skills that is the single determinant of investment advisor profitability in the current environment. Of course, skill sets like technical know-how and practice management also are essential. Nevertheless, without the marketing skills to find qualified

prospects, motivate them to take action and ensure a long-term relationship, the technical and practice management skill sets do not stand a chance to be used.

Based on our research on and our experience in consulting with elite financial advisors, we find that few advisors are currently marketing their services and expertise as effectively as they could. Even though high-end financial advisors do a lot of marketing, they still are not capitalizing on all of the opportunities available to them.

We have estimated this marketing gap to translate into revenues of $150,000 to more than $800,000 in a given year. When high-end financial advisors develop systematic marketing efforts, their revenues increase by 15% - 256%.

On a percentage basis, the marketing gap is even bigger among the less successful advisors. Investment advisors with fewer years in the business, whose practices are further away from the centers of influence, who are less technically expert or who are less skilled in managing their practices ,are often less proficient at marketing.

All investment advisors should expect to benchmark their marketing skills against the best of the best. These are exceptional financial services marketers—not sales professionals, marketers. We find these marketers among the elite financial advisors as well as among those who are fast tracking to this level.

After evaluating the way they work, we have been able to identify why they are more successful than the rest. The difference is they fill the marketing gap, and they do it with client-focused marketing plans.

Marketing Plans in Name Only

You probably have heard that you should have a marketing plan. You really should. Studies show that those investment advisors with a marketing plan tend to be more successful.

Why do marketing plans work? Let's consider how the overwhelming majority of investment advisors market their services. They go and look for business. While they employ a variety of prospecting strategies, we find that they are rarely organized or systematic in their efforts. They run hard but rarely run efficiently. Their success comes from the sheer intensity of their efforts. Now imagine how much more effective they would be if they took that intensity and married it to a systematic approach.

A well-conceived marketing plan works to create systematic activity. A good plan creates focus, accountability and an ability to evaluate progress.

The problem is that most marketing plans are marketing plans in name only. Too many marketing plans sit on the shelf all year. Typically, an investment advisor might write a marketing plan at the beginning of the year and not look at it again until the time comes to revise it. In between, investment advisors look for new business in the way they have always looked for new business.

It's no wonder marketing plans have a bad name among investment advisors. It's obvious that the broad-based marketing plan as traditionally constructed has a lot to be desired. A far better alternative is to create client-focused marketing plans, that is, a marketing plan for each top client.

The Client-Focused Marketing Plan Process

Instead of thinking broadly and writing a marketing plan dealing with all the strategic and tactical alternatives open to you, let's think more narrowly. Let's create marketing plans that lead to action — action that results in meaningful new investment advisory business.

One of the most effective and efficient ways to garner meaningful new investment advisory business is to leverage your relationships with your current wealthy clientele. Leveraging those relationships brings you to two goals. One goal is to expand the nature and amount of business you do with these selected clients. The other goal is to generate new business prospects through personal introductions and referrals from highly satisfied clients. Personal introductions and client referrals are the prospecting strategy of choice.

How can you achieve these two goals? You can accomplish this by employing the three steps of the Client-Focused Marketing Plan Process:

- Step #1: Evaluate your client base for the best opportunities to build your business.
- Step #2: Write client-focused marketing plans.
- Step #3: Integrate the client-focused marketing plans into a comprehensive marketing plan.

Step #1: Evaluate Your Client Base for the Best Opportunities to Build Your Business

The objective is to assess the financial potential of your current clients—especially your more affluent investor clients. Look for which clients are profitable and which ones are a drain on your resources. We have found that relatively few investment advisors take the time to evaluate the bottom-line profitability of any of their clients.

In addition, look for those clients who have increased revenue potential and identify the ones that do not. You will be ahead of the game in doing this as relatively few financial advisors have a solid feel for this issue. While many know there might be more business potential from a given client, few investment advisors have a clear vision about how they might capitalize on this potential. From a business-building perspective, to know if it is worth committing more resources to a client, you need to know what to expect in return.

Specifically, you need to know which clients will lead to wealthier and more successful prospects and which ones will not. As personal introductions and client referrals generally are the most effective prospecting approaches, it's necessary to have a sense of which of your current clients you should approach. We have found that this takes insight (such as high-net-worth psychology) as well as time and practice.

Along the same lines, you must determine what resources you have to dedicate to generating new business. For most financial advisors, it's impossible to capitalize on every opportunity. There are not enough resources. Rather, you have to balance the opportunities against the time and resources you have available.

In this step, you are identifying the best opportunities to build your business — those clients who you believe will lead to more business and more clients. The next step is to develop the individual client marketing plans.

Step #2: Write Client-Focused Marketing Plans

What we have found to work well is for you to keep a folder for each affluent client. The key document in the folder is the client-focused marketing plan. If you are technically inclined the folder will be stored on your computer. If you prefer paper this folder likely will take up a file drawer.

The client-focused marketing plan will be based on your extensive knowledge of your clients. Actually, we find that writing a client-focused marketing plan helps many investment advisors learn much more about their clients than they thought possible. Simply completing a fact-finder would help you establish such information as:

- General information
- Family information
- Advisors currently retained
- Assets
- Debt
- Business interests
- Business P&L and income statements
- Retirement plans
- Insurance holdings

Besides obtaining objective data via the fact-finder and examining documents, you also need to concentrate on the subjective data. Subjective data includes the client's values, feelings and goals.

You also need to specify the high-net-worth personality of the client. While high-net-worth psychology was developed for and has proven to be effective with the affluent, it also has been shown to be extremely useful when the clients would not yet be classified as affluent. The high-net-worth personality is instrumental in enabling you to most effectively customize your approach and when you want to take constructive actions to generate new business, a highly customized approach is only logical.

High-net-worth psychology also is highly effective in helping you best manage the relationship with your wealthy clients. One component of your client-focused marketing plan is to specify what actions you are going to take in order to significantly enhance your relationship with these clients.

It all comes together when you take this information and use it as the foundation for a marketing plan. By understanding the fact pattern and high-net-worth personality, you will be able to identify opportunities to do more business with a client. You will also become aware of who they will be able to introduce or refer you to. Once you are aware of all the opportunities—expanded business and personal introductions or referrals—you need to set up a timetable to detail the specific actions you need to take. In each client folder, you should have set out all your action steps that will result in more business for you.

In the end, you need to assign some numbers to each client-focused marketing plan. In other words, you need to specify a revenue potential number for each of these clients. That revenue number is based on the amount of continuing revenue, additional revenue from asset capture and the revenue due to referrals and personal introductions. We have found that after developing such comprehensive files on each of these clients, investment advisors are able to come close to predicting revenue numbers.

A few leading financial advisors have taken the entire approach up one level by incorporating expense numbers into their client-focused marketing plans. With expense estimates, they are able to make decisions on how to spend their time based on clearly articulated cost/benefit considerations.

It's important to remember that these client-focused marketing plans are always evolving. As you become more familiar with your affluent client situations, you will uncover new ways to build your business. In addition, as your clients' situations change or external forces impact their situations, you will be ready to quickly take action that will result in more business.

Step #3: Integrate the Client-Focused Marketing Plans into a Comprehensive Marketing Plan

With the first set of basic client-focused marketing plans in place, you can develop a comprehensive marketing plan for your practice. Using the individual plans as a base you can comfortably project future revenues.

The volume of these projected revenues will enable you to assess whether you need to expand your marketing efforts beyond those that are client-focused. For example, you may need to enhance relationships with advisors such as accountants and attorneys. However, we have found that the high-end investment advisors who have adopted the client-focused marketing approach have adapted it to developing business with other professional advisors. These investment advisors create individualized advisor-focused marketing plans.

When investment advisors first use the comprehensive approach, we find they initially project they will earn about 30% of their new revenues as a result of client-focused marketing plans and 70% from other activities. With some experience using this approach, we find they flip their projections and project that most of their new revenues will come from client-focused marketing plans. Why the change? Because the client-focused marketing plans produce the results for which they were looking.

Client-focused marketing plans open doors to new prospects. This in turn will move the financial advisor to concentrate his or her resources on even more revenue-generating opportunities.

"It's a kind of spiritual snobbery that makes people think they can be happy without money."

- Albert Camus

The client-focused marketing plan process is one of the most effective and efficient ways of creating a pipeline of increasingly wealthier and more successful clients. For investment advisors committed to building their businesses, this approach creates the structure—provides the systematic framework—to consistently generate new revenues.

We've all been around this business long enough to know there are no silver bullets, no one answer. The real answer is to figure out the things that do work and then do them on a consistent basis. We know client-focused marketing plans work. We also know that investment advisors are human, and can fall back to their old, less productive habits. Client-focused marketing plans are like any other tool. You need to use them habitually to see results.

282

1% Information, 99% Implementation

When we work with elite financial advisors we usually start by talking about what we know — the kind of information in this book. We go over the research and present the data. We cull the hundreds of studies and surveys we have conducted over the years for the best insights.

Using our data and the experience of the advisor we agree on what is happening in the high-net-worth market. We come to a common understanding of the psychology of the affluent investor, on who the key competitors are and what they are doing and the significant trends. Then we work on the implications for the business of the financial advisors and create tactical plans.

These steps are both necessary, and easy.

The most difficult step is implementation. Success is 1% information and 99% implementation. The brilliance of a strategy fades away if it is followed by poor execution.

The information is the science. Implementation is the art.

From Science to Art

High-net-worth psychology is predicated on science. All the findings we report are statistically significant, valid and accurate. The research methodology we employ is state-of-the-art. Because of the academic foundation of Prince & Associates LLC and the rigorousness demanded by our peers in academia and our clients (e.g., *Institutional Investor/Private Asset Management*) our research needs to meet strict standards.

> ***"Invention is 1% inspiration and 99% perspiration."***
>
> ***- Thomas Edison***

We initially built a successful management consulting practice based solely on information. Our expertise in selected areas—the financial behavior of the affluent, the best practices of elite financial advisors and our databases on the private wealth industry worldwide—proved to be in demand by financial institutions and investment advisors alike.

But, in today's competitive environment, information is not enough. In fact, it's a very small part of success, just about 1%.

As we worked with elite financial advisors, we found they were very interested in the information, but they were even more interested in applying the information to build their businesses. Elite financial

advisors are focused on implementation. They looked at high-net-worth psychology and, because of their extensive experience, knew that we were not only on the mark, but had also opened new opportunities for them.

Although our information is meaningful in and of itself, information alone is never enough for elite financial advisors. They want to convert information into activity that generates business. Hence we moved into implementation.

We also found that leading financial institutions wanted more than just information. They, too, began seeking help in implementing the insights. They became interested in converting the information into programs that improved the bottom line.

Information is necessary, but insufficient. The move must be made from insight to action. Implementation makes the difference, it grows the bottom line. It is the 99% that translates into success.

We've been lucky to work with some of the finest advisors in the financial services industry. In consulting to some of the leading financial institutions as well, we've seen how to apply high-net-worth psychology to significantly improve business.

Most of the credit for these bottom-line results is due to the advisors who have taken the time to learn high-net-worth psychology and adopt it. Remember, high-net-worth psychology is an approach to being successful with affluent investors. It's a way of ensuring that you are focusing on what's really important to them. It has helped some of the most successful investment advisors become even more successful because it is a system. As such, it helps you to do what you do well, and to do it consistently. Such consistency is the way to build a top-flight investment advisory business.

> ***"Small opportunities are often the beginning of great enterprises."***
> ***- Demosthenes***

We have worked with some of the finest investment advisors throughout the world. We have seen their unsurpassed innovation and incomparable drive. We have seen their deep concern and commitment to their clients. We have also come to recognize that many investment advisors are held back only because they have not yet made the decision to excel.

Without question, often it is not easy to change the way you work. It's even more difficult when you are already achieving a measure of success. Still, we have yet to find an investment advisor who said he

or she can not do better. High-net-worth psychology should be viewed as a framework, an approach, a system to help you do better.

We understand what it takes for an investment advisor to succeed in the high-net-worth market. Of the many investment advisors working today, only a portion will be eminently successful. You can be among the ranks of elite financial advisors. You just have to commit to excel.